Praise for *God Loves the Autistic Mind*

"I was high-fiving the angels the whole time I read this brilliant insider view of autistic sanctity and prayer life. Fr. Matthew has given us an enchiridion on autistic prayer, with insightful, relatable devotions. Not only are our autistic ways of praying not barriers to God's presence and mercy, but Fr. Matthew shows the robust possibilities of autistic prayer, sanctity, and mission. He has applied *lex credendi, lex orandi* to autism perfectly. I'm going to buy copies for everyone I know."

—Summer Kinard, MDiv, ThM, author of
Of Such is the Kingdom: A Practical Theology of Disability

"What a blessing this is! With wisdom, compassion, and clear-eyed faith, Fr. Schneider—himself a priest on the autism spectrum—has given the world something wonderful: a book that will bring consolation and hope to countless people with autism and all those who love them. Both practical and prayerful, Fr. Schneider's work will open minds, shatter myths, and touch hearts."

—Deacon Greg Kandra, journalist and author of
The Busy Person's Guide to Prayer

"As an autistic priest and missionary to the autism community, Fr. Matthew Schneider shares insights on communicating with God in a way comfortable for the autistic mind. Through the spiritual disciplines, we on the spectrum can unite with

God in heart and mind. *God Loves the Autistic Mind* is filled with inspiring accounts of autistics' journeys of faith. Fr. Matthew provides fifty-two devotions to enrich our faith and communion with God. As a theologian and minister with autism, I highly recommend *God Loves the Autistic Mind* to those who desire an intimate relationship with the Father and have a passion for inclusion."

—Ron Sandison, author of *Views from the Spectrum*
and founder of Spectrum Inclusion

"Fr. Matthew Schneider, LC, has brought together a cornucopia of autistic experiences of prayer, not only drawing on his personal experience but also citing a rich array of historical and contemporary Christians. No two autistic people will pray alike, but many will find something to identify with here. His introduction to autism, Christian faith, and prayer will not disappoint those who rejoice in footnotes or references, but should prove equally accessible to anyone approaching this subject for the first time. Thoroughly recommended."

—AspiePriest, autistic diocesan priest and blogger

"Fr. Matthew P. Schneider does a great job laying out a prayer method aimed at those with autism who are independent or nearly so. Fr. Schneider explains in a clear and convincing manner how certain features of autism can be helpful in developing a strong prayer life, and he also addresses those features that can make prayer difficult. He adapts the traditional method of Lectio Divina and makes it concrete with prayers that speak not only to the heart but also to the mind."

—David Rizzo, author of *Faith, Family, and Children with Special Needs*
and *Praying for Your Special Needs Child*

"*God Loves the Autistic Mind* is the first of its kind: a book that focuses on authentically helping autistic people (who are often overlooked in churches) in their prayer lives—from the autistic perspective. I believe any autistic Christian can benefit from giving this book a read and engaging in the meditations that speak to them."

—Stephanie Bethany, autistic YouTuber

"As a cleric who works clinically with individuals with autism, I search for meaningful and effective tools that individuals on the autism spectrum can access. I am especially interested in prayer, because when I work with men studying to become priests and deacons, there seem to be so few resources. And there are often so many hurdles for these individuals to wade through. The forms of prayer offered through Fr. Schneider's book offer not only additional tangible methods, but hope from one who is there.

"We need more of this type of work and I am grateful to Fr. Matthew for the courage to write it."

—Deacon Lawrence R. Sutton, Ph.D., author of *How to Welcome, Include, and Catechize Children with Autism and Other Special Needs: A Parish-Based Approach* and *Teaching Students with Autism in a Catholic Setting*

GOD LOVES
THE AUTISTIC MIND

PRAYER GUIDE FOR THOSE
ON THE SPECTRUM
AND THOSE WHO LOVE US

FR. MATTHEW P. SCHNEIDER, LC

Pauline
BOOKS & MEDIA

Boston

Library of Congress Control Number: 2021946285
CIP data is available.

ISBN 0-8198-3162-X
ISBN 978-0-8198-3162-0

Imprimi Potest: Reverend Shawn Aaron, LC
            January 22, 2022

Every effort has been made to trace copyright holders and to obtain their permission for the use of copyright material. The publisher apologizes for any errors or omissions and would be grateful if notified of any corrections that should be incorporated in future reprints or editions of this book.

Many manufacturers and sellers distinguish their products through the use of trademarks. Any trademark designations that appear in this book are used in good faith but are not authorized by, associated with, or sponsored by the trademark owners.

Scripture quotations are from the *Revised Standard Version of the Bible—Second Catholic Edition* (Ignatius Edition), copyright © 2006, National Council of the Churches of Christ in the United States of America. Used by permission. All rights reserved.

Excerpts from the English translation of the *Catechism of the Catholic Church* for use in the United States of America, copyright © 1994, United States Catholic Conference, Inc. — Libreria Editrice Vaticana. Used with permission. English translation of the *Catechism of the Catholic Church*: Modifications from the Editio Typica copyright © 1997, United States Conference of Catholic Bishops—Libreria Editrice Vaticana.

Excerpt from the English *Translation of The Order of Celebrating Matrimony*, copyright © 2013, The International Commission on English in the Liturgy Corporation. Used by permission.

Excerpts from papal and magsterium texts © Libreria Editrice Vaticana. Used by permission. All rights reserved.

Cover design by Ryan McQuade

Published by Pauline Books & Media, 50 Saint Pauls Avenue, Boston, MA 02130-3491

Printed in the U.S.A.

www.pauline.org

Pauline Books & Media is the publishing house of the Daughters of St. Paul, an international congregation of women religious serving the Church with the communications media.

1 2 3 4 5 6 7 8 9   26 25 24 23 22

Contents

PART ONE

What Makes Autistic Prayer Different?

Chapter One

Chapter Two

PART TWO

52 Meditations for Autistics and Those Who Love Us

Introduction

"JESUS LOVES YOU just the way you are" is a common refrain in CCD or religious education classes. However, those of us living with an autistic brain don't often feel it. We feel more like an outsider in social groups, including in church. In fact, we are nearly twice as likely as anyone else (1.84 times) to never attend church, and not attending church is more likely for us than for persons with any other condition.[1] Also, autistics are significantly more likely to be atheists and agnostics, or to make their own religious system.[2]

---

1 See Andrew L. Whitehead, "Religion and Disability: Variation in Religious Service Attendance Rates for Children with Chronic Health Conditions," *Journal for the Scientific Study of Religion* 57, no. 2 (2018): 377–95, https://doi.org/10.1111/jssr.12521. As compared in this study, those with the following conditions were more likely to attend church at least occasionally: ADD/ADHD, developmental delay, learning disability, oppositional defiant disorder, depression, anxiety, speech problems, hearing problems and a brain injury.

2 See Catherine Caldwell-Harris et al., "Religious Belief Systems of Persons with High Functioning Autism" (CogSci 2011, Online: Cognitive Science Journal Archive, 2011), 3362–66, http://csjarchive.cogsci.rpi.edu/proceedings/2011/papers/0782/paper0782.pdf.

At the same time evidence seems to show that religion helps families with autistic members have a better life. A 2015 study on families with teenage autistic children noted, "We found strength of religious faith to be a significant predictor of FQOL [Family Quality of Life]."[3]

In fact, summarizing all the previous research on this topic, a researcher in 2019 concluded, "For many parents of children diagnosed with ASD, religion is a means of coping that endures. The importance of religion appears to continue throughout the lifespan, while other sources of support may wane in significance."[4] A 1999 study in Ireland quoted many parents of autistic children: "I always prayed, it helped me cope"; "I prayed all the time, my faith kept me going"; "Prayer was the only thing that helped"; "Prayer helps, I would have gone crackers if I didn't pray"; "Even though I was mad with God I still kept praying"; and "Prayer is all we have at the end of the day."[5]

---

[3] Thomas L. Boehm, Erik W. Carter, and Julie Lounds Taylor, "Family Quality of Life During the Transition to Adulthood for Individuals With Intellectual Disability and/or Autism Spectrum Disorders," *American Journal on Intellectual and Developmental Disabilities* 120, no. 5 (September 1, 2015): 395–411, https://doi.org/10.1352/1944-7558-120.5.395.

[4] Susan L. Moerschbacher, "An Exploration of Parental Perceptions of Inclusive Services and Supports Provided by Faith Communities for Children Diagnosed with Autism and Their Families" (Doctor of Education, Lakeland, FL, Southeastern University, 2019), 18–19, https://firescholars.seu.edu/cgi/viewcontent.cgi?article=1042&context=coe.

[5] Patricia Coulthard and Michael Fitzgerald, "In God We Trust? Organised Religion and Personal Beliefs as Resources and Coping Strategies, and Their Implications for Health in Parents with a Child on the Autistic Spectrum," *Mental Health, Religion & Culture* 2, no. 1 (May 1, 1999): 30, https://doi.org/10.1080/13674679908406329.

Prayer should be a practice that unites Christians, but unfortunately how it is presented is not always the most helpful for those of us with differently structured brains. Some things we struggle with and some things we just process differently. There is even an autistic tendency to be better at some things. Thus, autistic Christians will tend to pray differently from non-autistic Christians. This is not a critique of either way. It's not unlike the way men and women tend to pray differently. Both are good and there is overlap, but tendencies arise in both that are worth exploring.

The goal of this book is to help my fellow autistic Christians and their families pray better. I think this is the first book that explains autistic prayer and offers devotions to autistics from the inside. Other books I have seen on the topic were written from the outside, whether by a parent or by a researcher.

Prayer is always an adventure. Autistic prayer is no different: it is just a different type of adventure. It's as if everyone else is watching Star Wars while we're watching Star Trek. Both are space adventures with interstellar travel, warp speed, and laser weapons, but the rules for how things work are a little different. Each person must go on his or her own adventure seeking out God in prayer. This book provides something of a roadmap or interstellar guide for the autistic seeking Jesus, but it cannot replace your own effort.

One of the difficulties with autism is that autistic brains are quite diverse. Neurotypical individuals have a standard system of connectivity. Scientists can see this in an MRI. However, when they looked at autistic brains in the same scans, they were all different from the neurotypical brains, but also from each other, such that researchers couldn't even figure out a good way to group them.[6] This reminds us of the adage, "If you've seen one autistic, you've seen one autistic." For the purposes of this book, I will have to admit that this means most autistics will not identify with every point. I don't even experience every point I mention. I have studied numerous testimonies from autistic teens, men, and women to try to understand some of the diversity we have experienced with different realities or aspects of prayer. Thus, don't worry if one section of the book does not correspond to your experience of prayer: just use the parts that help you.

The book is divided into two parts. Part One is an autistic guide to prayer in a more systematic way, and will cover types of prayer, how prayer deepens, and a few prayer myths. Part Two consists of individual devotions for prayer or meditation. Before going on, I want to make two notes in this introduction that will give a bit of perspective to what follows: a brief autobiography, and a note about language. If you are not familiar with autism, I'd also suggest reading Appendix A: What Is Autism.

My Life as an Autistic Priest

I always knew something was different with me. I did well in school and was near the top of my class in engineering, but I struggled in other areas. Before being diagnosed, I'd sometimes said, "I left engineering, but engineering never left me." Then, in late 2015, I did about a dozen hours of extensive testing and, in January 2016,

---

6 See Avital Hahamy, Marlene Behrmann, and Rafael Malach, "The Idiosyncratic Brain: Distortion of Spontaneous Connectivity Patterns in Autism Spectrum Disorder," *Nature Neuroscience* 18, no. 2 (February 2015): 302–9, https://doi.org/10.1038/nn.3919.

received a diagnosis of autism spectrum disorder, noting that the diagnosis would have been Asperger's in prior diagnostic manuals that distinguished them. I was initially devastated. However, within a short while, that changed, and I realized I was better off now knowing, and I should be open about this to live in peace and to help others like me.

I never fit in. I was always the exception in school where I got above average grades and rarely got in trouble. However, I'd come right home after school and read the same books over and over. I could always see patterns. Even today when driving, I will notice things like patterns of license plate numbers: I constantly do math with their digits.

In elementary school, I had wretched handwriting. My coordination was always bad. As a kid, I rarely won *Street Fighter II* against my friends. In computer engineering, I was the slowest typist in the class. Even in the seminary, my handwriting was so bad that my formators told me that I needed to improve. Back in elementary school, a specialist was hired to come in and investigate what could be causing my bad handwriting. All I remember is that at the end she wasn't able to help me because I had above average IQ and my reaction times on tests were about average. In hindsight, it's obvious to me that if the current diagnostic standards were in place, I would have been referred for an autism diagnosis after that meeting.

Instead, I went through high school with low-level honors, studied two years of computer engineering, entered a seminary, went through three psychological examinations at different times, and was ordained a priest, all without ever knowing I was autistic. When occasionally I would hear brief descriptions of Asperger's in the media, I thought it a slight personality trait, not a radically different way to see the world. A few times I'd thought, "Oh, maybe I'm like that."

When I was first ordained a priest, I was assigned as a chaplain at a school for three years. However, after a year, I was surprised that they didn't want me back. I knew I hadn't been perfect, but I thought the small mistakes were well within the normal learning curve of a new job. Someone suggested Asperger's and my superiors sent me back to study part time the next fall while working behind the scenes for the national office. In hindsight, it is very clear that misreading social cues—as an autistic is apt to do—was the primary issue.

The intervening summer, I did some tests, mentioning beforehand that I might have "Asperger's" to the psychologist, but he just did general tests such as the MMPI (Minnesota Multiphasic Personality Inventory). In hindsight, none of these tests would be any good for discovering autism. The MMPI is not designed for diagnosing autism and the research seems to say we are slightly different from neurotypical controls but not that distinct. This psychologist did diagnose me with depression, which, after feeling stretched as a school chaplain then getting kicked out for reasons I didn't then understand, is not surprising. Later on, in reading and hindsight I think I was also depressed for part of middle school from all the teasing and bullying. I'm guessing that might sound familiar to other autistics.

A year later, someone suggested I try another psychologist to see about autism or Asperger's. I was rather hesitant at first as I thought that had been dismissed, but I figured I could go through with it. As noted above, in January 2016, I received a formal diagnosis.

Along with the evident issues of coordination related to my handwriting and reading social signals that nixed my time as a school chaplain, I am autistic in other ways too. Some are ways that others consider negative, such as my irregular sensory input, certain executive functioning issues, stress and anxiety. As far as senses, I am hyposensitive and hypersensitive in different ways. I am hyposensitive such that my room is super-bright and regarding food flavor where I often load on garlic or tabasco. On the other hand, I am hypersensitive about food texture—I joke about hating kale but, honestly, it's the plasticky texture, not the taste. As far as sound goes, I can't regulate it very much, so I need something moderate (neither too much nor too little). As far as executive functioning, I can only accomplish things because of whiteboards, Google Calendar and my "to do" app. If I don't write out everything I need to do for the week in a plan at the beginning of the week, I will get almost zilch done. In such a case, every responsibility will weigh down on me and I'll be anxiously stuck at my desk for hours getting basically nothing done. Because of all the above reasons, I easily tend to get over-stressed and anxious. I often use stim toys and appreciate the weighted blanket on my bed.

At the same time, being autistic gives me some advantages: long-term memory of facts, pattern recognition, and concentration are the most evident. My long-term memory is so good that my nickname in seminary was Schneider-pedia, or they would joke that Wikipedia checks with me first. I can honestly say that even though I finished formal study of philosophy fifteen years ago, I could still probably pass the exams—it took me a while even to realize that was unusual. I just thought people remembered. I often remember with such precision that I've had to learn to round numbers off to not sound weird to neurotypicals: in most cases neurotypicals prefer I say, "about 60" rather than "63." I don't really understand why this is, but I adapt out of charity. Likewise, I am very good at pattern recognition. I often see patterns in things that others miss and this has helped me become one of the most followed Catholic priests on social media (I have over 50,000 Twitter followers). A lot of this pattern recognition is automatic in a way that I find difficult to explain to others—I figure this is a large part of why I haven't been super successful at helping others grow big online followings when they asked for tips. In the same vein, I think I use that part of my brain rather than the neurotypical face-recognition circuit to recognize faces, but I am still not the best at that. Finally, if I'm into something, I concentrate very deeply. People don't believe me when I say I've never fallen asleep studying, but that's the honest truth.

Overall, I am very happy as a priest, with both the positive traits of autism and some extra autistic challenges. I'm also happy that I do an intellectual ministry where I can focus more on the strengths and am held down less by the challenges.

Language and Perspective

This book is intended for us autistics and our family, friends, teachers, or allies. As such, you may have noted my consistent use of "autistic" over "person with autism."

Saying "autistic" is called identity-first language. This is how most of us with such brains prefer to be called, by margins of between 2:1 and 4:1 depending on the survey.[7] It is primarily

---

7 I cite several surveys in this post: Matthew Schneider, "Christians, Please Call Us Autistic, Blind, and Deaf," *Through Catholic Lenses* (blog), October 17, 2019, https://www.patheos.com/blogs/throughcatholiclenses/2019/10/christians-please-call-us-autistic-blind-and-deaf/.

about a different brain. It is like I am 6-foot-3-inch male and Caucasian—I can't change any of these three without ceasing to be me. Something one "has" sounds external and changeable as in I have an ASUS laptop I'm writing this on, but in a few years, I'll likely buy a different brand. Some things we have may be closer to our person than that, but still somewhat external, and not changing who we are: once I had black hair, as I dyed it, even though I now have light brown hair, and in a few years will have gray hair. Autism is part of who I am, not something external.

You will note, nonetheless, that I respect authors I quote and leave "person with autism" or person-first language if the author uses it. I also respect the minority of individuals on the spectrum who prefer it.

I use the word "autistic" as I would use a national or language signifier. I might say I am a Canadian living in the U.S.A. or an autistic living in a neurotypical world. In most communities with disabilities, person-first language—"person with disabilities"—is preferred. However, all three groups that have strong preferences for identity first—the blind, the Deaf and the autistic—are groups that due to their disability communicate in a different manner akin to a different language. The difference in autistic language is not as evident as it is for the blind or the Deaf, but our reading of body language and often of connotative meanings of phrases (like using irony to say the opposite of what you mean) are very different for us. In a sense my native language is autistic English: it has the same vocabulary as standard English, and words mean the same things denotatively; but some connotations and non-verbal communication are different. For example, we tend to take words more literally when people mean them analogously, and we tend not to look people in the eye even when being deep and honest.

Throughout the book I simply use "Autistics," but this includes those with various other diagnoses, including Asperger's, PDD-NOS (Pervasive Developmental Disorder-Not Otherwise Specified), and CDD (Childhood Disintegrative Disorder). Currently in the DSM-5 (the fifth edition of the *Diagnostic and Statistical Manual of Mental Disorders*, which sets diagnostic standards for psychological conditions in the USA and Canada) there is one diagnosis, autism spectrum disorder (ASD), while previous manuals split this into several. As such, by the current psychological diagnosis we are all Autistics. (In other countries, the standard is not the DSM-5, but rather the ICD-10 [the tenth revision of the *International Statistical Classification of Diseases and Related Health Problems* from the World Health Organization]. The ICD-10 still distinguishes Asperger's from autism, although it notes that they are related, and that the differences are not in the most fundamental aspects.) Nonetheless, I understand those who were diagnosed with Asperger's and want to keep that identity. In such a case, just mentally replace "autistics" with "Aspies."

At times I use "neurotypicals" to describe people whose brains function like those of the majority of human beings. Differently functioning brains have different advantages and disadvantages, so I avoid saying "better" or "normal" in this regard. If I use neurodiverse, I mean not only autistics but others with unusual brains that can be advantageous at times but disadvantageous at other times, such as bipolar, OCD, or ADHD individuals.

I use a lot of Catholic vocabulary, but I try to explain terms I suspect some might not understand. People come to this at different levels of such knowledge, and I have tried to accommodate most. If some Catholic term still seems hard to grasp, I recommend the dictionary Father John Hardon composed, which is searchable online;[8] this tends to have clear, brief definitions, while most other resources read more like encyclopedia entries.

---

8 www.catholicculture.org/culture/library/dictionary.

PART ONE

What Makes Autistic Prayer Different?

WE AUTISTICS OFTEN struggle in certain aspects of prayer but can be very good at other aspects. Autism relates to prayer life in many ways. We also pray about our life's triumphs and difficulties, which likely vary a bit for us. The soul is the core of prayer and every human has a soul of the same type with equal dignity. However, our emotions and brain processes are also involved in prayer since we exist as a union of body and soul. Autistic brains and emotions are structured differently than those of neuro-typicals.

I want to present a way for those of us on the spectrum to learn to pray, and to pray about the things we deal with. I don't think the method needs to be so radically different from that of traditional prayer guides, but it needs some adaptation to be applicable to our neurology. I don't think this book will answer every question or deal with every diversity on the spectrum, but I hope it can help us to pray and help others to pray with us.

The first two chapters in this part will cover prayer systematically. Chapter One covers some types of prayer and how autistics might be involved in each type. Chater Two covers autistics going deeper into mental prayer and contemplation.

CHAPTER ONE

Types of Autistic Prayer

THERE ARE DIFFERENT ways to categorize prayer. The *Catechism* (2644) notes one division: "blessing, petition, intercession, thanksgiving, and praise." This is a helpful way of dividing prayer by the goal (or proximate end) of that prayer. This subdivision is discussed in many books on prayer. However, this division will be demonstrated in the devotions later rather than systematically here.

Instead of dividing by goals, I want to examine the division by forms of prayer. A form is more about how someone prays: each form here can match any of the five goals above. This chapter will discuss vocal prayer (including liturgical prayer), stimming and prayer, location or objects in prayer, and mental prayer.

Vocal Prayer and Liturgy

If asked to name a prayer, most Catholics would give answers like the Our Father, the Rosary, the Hail Mary, the Saint Michael prayer, or the Mass. All of these are vocal prayers, as they follow a set formula of words that is repeated. Vocal prayer refers to a prayer where a specific predetermined set of words is said aloud or in silence.[9]

Vocal prayers, however, are not magical incantations. We need our spiritual mind and heart to accompany these words: they give the prayer meaning for us and set our desires towards them. When praying the Rosary, you may think on each word, let your spiritual mind and heart focus on the mystery, such as the visitation, or focus on the intention for which you are praying, such as hoping grandma's surgery goes well. All of these are prayer. However, simply saying prayers to get them done—for example, so mom will take you out for ice cream—is not praying well. Vocal prayer for any Christian should help the interior dialogue with God. In fact, the *Catechism* says the following about vocal prayer: "It is most important that the heart should be present to him to whom we are speaking in prayer."[10]

In this section, I will speak of the comfort of continuity, verbal stim prayers, and liturgical prayers.

Many autistics find that repetition and continuity are satisfying. Since I entered religious life in 2001, every single morning I've said the same five-minute morning prayer with only one significant change in two decades. This gives me a continuity of the first thing I do every morning beyond personal hygiene and dressing. As a priest, I also pray the Mass and Liturgy of the Hours each day: although many parts vary, they maintain the same structure. For

---

9 For a selection of prayers, see Appendix B, page 197.
10 CCC 2700.

example, each hour of the Liturgy of the Hours begins with a hymn, followed by psalms, a reading, and a closing prayer.

This comfort can help us realize that God is asking us to respond to him in an autistic manner. If repeating a certain prayer helps unite me with God in mind and heart, it is a good prayer. The fact that simultaneously the repetition and familiarity calm my neurology is a bonus. It gives me comfort that God wants me to communicate with him in a way I am more comfortable with.

Some prayers are so short they can almost become a stim. Stimming is behavior consisting of repetitive movements, actions, words, sounds, etc., that we autistics often use for various ends like sensory or emotional regulation, or for expressing emotions. The following, although short, are complete prayers:

1. "My Jesus, mercy."
2. "Jesus, Son of the living God, have mercy on me, a sinner."
3. "In the name of the Father, and of the Son, and of the Holy Spirit."
4. "Holy Mary, Mother of God, pray for us sinners, now and at the hour of our death."
5. "My hope is the Father, my refuge is the Son, my shelter is the Holy Ghost, O Holy Trinity, glory unto you."
6. "O Lady [Mary], by the love which you bear to Jesus, help me to love him."
7. "For the sake of his sorrowful passion, have mercy on us and on the whole world."

These prayers go back in Christian history. The first four have such an ancient origin that the author is unknown. The last three are attributed to: (5) Saint Ioannikios the Great (an Eastern-rite saint living in modern-day Turkey from 752–846), (6) Saint

Bridget of Sweden (1303–1375), and (7) Saint Faustina Kowalska (1905–1938).

Each of these seven prayers can be said in the time of a single breath, even if prayed slowly or in a meditative manner. In fact, in Eastern Christian practice, it is suggested that the Jesus Prayer (number 2 above) be said in two parts, first as we breathe in and then as we breathe out, such that one is able to fulfil the biblical command to "pray constantly" (1 Thess 5:17).

The names of Jesus or Mary said with reverence can be an even shorter prayer than those listed above. Such quick prayers can be said repeatedly and keep uniting us to Our Lord and Savior. This kind of verbal stim praying will not work for all autistics, but I think it works for enough to be mentioned here.

Then we move on to liturgical prayer. The liturgy is a special form of vocal prayer where we encounter God's presence in the sacraments. The regularity and schedule of Catholic Mass often helps those of us with executive functioning difficulties where we like sameness. A few strategies exist for parishes to accommodate or include us. Here I want to mention ideas for us to live it better. The liturgy, especially Mass or events like eucharistic processions, require us to participate together with others and often require exposing ourselves to sensory irritants. This can be a challenge.

First, we should distinguish what is part of the liturgy—and thus essential—from what is good for accompanying the liturgy but can be skipped if need be. The liturgy we are obliged to attend lasts from when the priest and other ministers process into the sanctuary to when they process out. Oftentimes parishes might warm up with a song before Mass and have a social after Mass. If the social and sensory situation is difficult for you, you can either prepare for and deal with these, or skip them by arriving right on time and then leaving right away. You can prepare for and deal with a social hour in various ways: having a role like carrying around the coffee to offer refills, making scripts, or setting a limit on your interaction with new people while focusing on those you already know. Neither going to nor skipping social hour is immoral, so don't feel guilty either way.

Second, it is valuable to prepare yourself and give yourself an easy sensory time before Mass if you might be overwhelmed. For many of us, Sunday Mass is going to be one of the more difficult things we do every week regarding social interaction and sensory issues.

Third, we need to keep ourselves focused on Jesus. We need to do it out of love for him and offer our sacrifices for his sake. When we love someone, we can do some acts beyond the ordinary to be with them, to please them. If participating at Mass is tough on us socially or sensorially, we can consider it the cross that Jesus gives us to take up.

Hopefully these ideas can help you live vocal prayer well. I think some of the individual devotions farther on will also help with these prayers.

Stimming and Prayer

We stim, yes, we do; stimming is what we do. Although I will critique William Stillman later, he makes an interesting note about stimming based on the research of Dr. Andrew Newberg. Stillman notes that people who are calm and focused in a meditative manner have a different blood flow to the brain. He also notes that repetitive movements similar to the stimming of autistics also tend to create similar patterns of blood flow in the brain.[11] This is not the depths of prayer, but I'm just noting that stimming and the like can help us with the initial stages of focusing ourselves for prayer.

I think we can integrate stimming and praying. God gave us our neurology with the need to stim, but he also allows that same stimming to help us come to him. Spiritual writers encourage us to involve the whole body in prayer. When we kneel we put ourselves in a position of respect to God, or when we raise our eyes we also often raise our spiritual hearts to God.

Most people think of being very still when they pray. Most images indicate a still posture, sitting or kneeling. One may even quote the psalmist: "Be still, and know that I am God" (Ps 46:10). However, I think it is valuable to take one step deeper to see that the purpose for this is to calm oneself. So, if we are calmer and more focused when stimming, we are more fully living Christian prayer as an autistic than if we were just still but less calm and focused.

In the *Spiritual Exercises*, Saint Ignatius speaks of prayer posture. He notes, "To enter on the contemplation now on my knees, now prostrate on the earth, now lying face upwards, now seated, now standing, always intent on seeking what I want."[12] This means that one should keep the posture that helps one rest in the Lord. In fact, a Vatican letter on prayer summarized this paragraph of

---

11 See William Stillman, *Autism and the God Connection: Redefining the Autistic Experience Through Extraordinary Accounts of Spiritual Giftedness*, Kindle (Naperville, IL: Sourcebooks, 2006), chap. two: Surrendering to Serendipity.

12 St. Ignatius of Loyola, *The Spiritual Exercises of St. Ignatius of Loyola*, trans. Elder Mullan (New York: P.J. Kennedy & Sons, 1914), 48 (par. 76), https://archive.org/details/spiritualexercis00ignauoft.

Ignatius as, "His body [the body of the one praying] should also take up the position most suited to recollection."[13]

Origen offers a lengthy description on preparing oneself for prayer and letting go of distractions. He notes that "one who is about to enter upon prayer ought first to have paused awhile and prepared himself to engage in prayer throughout more earnestly and intently, to have cast aside every distraction and confusion of thought."[14]

For Origen, the purpose of posture and stillness is clearly to remove distractions and focus the mind. In describing postures, he makes exceptions if one is injured, but notes that even the injured person should have the same disposition, reminding us that the purpose of any posture is to dispose the mind and heart toward prayer.

Thus, what we should do in prayer is position our bodies to best be focused and calm. Although most often neurotypicals do this by being still, this may not be the case for us. Instead, stimming focuses and calms us. This can apply to any kind of stimming. I find most often vestibular stimming (a system that gives us balance and spatial orientation) like rocking in a chair or pacing, is most helpful to me. However, many others on the spectrum might find flapping or spinning a fidget spinner to be more helpful.

---

13 Joseph Ratzinger, "Letter to the Bishops of the Catholic Church on Some Aspects of Christian Meditation—*Orationis Formas*," October 15, 1989, para. 26, https://www.vatican.va/roman_curia/congregations/cfaith/documents/rc_con_cfaith_doc_19891015_meditazione-cristiana_en.html.

14 Origen, *On Prayer*, trans. William A. Curtis (Grand Rapids, MI: Christian Classics Ethereal Library, 2001), chap. XX, https://ccel.org/ccel/origen/prayer/prayer.

We should feel completely comfortable stimming while praying. Stimming can often help us pray better. As autistic Christians, we can fully embrace the habit of stimming, making it part of our prayer routine. In fact, our stimming can even be a way to pray. Saint Charles de Foucauld defines prayer thus: "To pray is to be with God."[15] Being with God means being with him in our full autistic self. Our full autistic self includes being a person who stims.

The *Catechism* (2562) speaks about how our gestures and actions can become prayer: "Whether prayer is expressed in words or gestures, it is the whole man who prays." Many autistics feel like we can't stim except in more socially acceptable ways, except with those closest to us. Stimming before the Lord indicates that we trust him as a close confidant, not as a distant God.

Obviously, in more public prayer such as at Mass or in adoration with several others, less distracting stims would be preferred out of charity. If you are in the back row and silently stim with a stress ball or fidget spinner, that should not distract others, but verbal or noisy stims would be a distraction to the others in their prayer.

The Vatican letter on prayer does give one warning about certain postures that I think applies also to stimming. It says, "Some physical exercises automatically produce a feeling of quiet and relaxation, pleasing sensations, perhaps even phenomena of light and of warmth, which resemble spiritual well-being. To take such

---

15 Charles de Foucauld, *Spiritual Autobiography of Charles de Foucauld*, ed. Jean-François Six, trans. J. Holland Smith (New York: P. J. Kennedy & Sons, 1964), 85.

feelings for the authentic consolations of the Holy Spirit would be a totally erroneous way of conceiving the spiritual life."[16] In a similar way, although stimming in prayer calms and focuses us, this calmness and focus is not in itself the goal of Christian prayer. Christian prayer is meant to be a relationship. Stimming prepares us to talk with God and demonstrates our closeness to God. Although God can grant a deeper peace when we are in prayer and stimming, it would be a mistake to take the calmness coming from our stimming directly as God's action or peace.

Prayer of Location or Object

Along with stimming, I think two related aspects of prayer play a larger role in our prayer than in neurotypical prayer: location and objects. Such aids as a prayer corner, a pilgrimage, a rosary, or an image are obviously part of neurotypical prayer, but I think they can have an extra importance for us.

In my religious community we do a half-day morning retreat once a month. When I've had to do this on my own, I've found that visiting a nearby shrine helps me pray far more than simply grabbing some books or meditations at home. I would get up, eat breakfast, and drive somewhere to pray. When I lived just outside D.C., I drove up at least twice to Emmitsburg, where there are the shrines of Lourdes and Saint Elizabeth Ann Seton. Even while I've been writing this book, we had a morning retreat where the last two hours were left for praying on our own. To get another

---

16 Ratzinger, *Orationis Formas*, para. 28.

location to pray at, I drove a few minutes to a historical village nearby where I knew the grounds were open and all the buildings were closed on Mondays. Even in my house, I find I often need to specify a location for prayer versus other things. I often have a place where I pace (vestibular stimming). I even have my room divided into three parts: for sleeping, working (like typing this), and praying.

I think that being autistic makes us more sensitive to places we pray in. We may not be able to go on an international pilgrimage due to sensory issues, but often I think local sights like a grotto to Mary in the woods help autistic prayer immensely. When the place is more localized, we can often get attached to it.

That same attachment also leads to the importance of prayer objects. I know that for over a decade I consistently have used the same images of Jesus and Mary for prayer. Back in about 2008 or 2009, I was at a center in Cincinnati and noticed that they had a nice set of images on pressboard from the Men of the Sacred Heart that were about 6 by 8 inches. I got a set and took them with me for years as I transferred all around the world. Almost a decade later I happened to be back in Cincinnati, so I got an exact replica, since the originals were starting to get worn. I laminated the copy but often still like the originals. I can hold them anywhere from arms-length to pressing against my head in prayer. I still regularly pray with these images.

With our attachments to objects, we can really designate spaces for prayer and non-prayer. I think the repeated use of a particular object for prayer often helps to remind us of Jesus and separate our dedicated prayer time from other time. I find that sometimes we can easily connect a certain object to a certain task or a certain person. For example, if saying our rosary is connected to the activity of prayer or the persons of Jesus and Mary, it can be a huge help to our prayer.

Summer Kinard wrote a whole guide to making a space for prayer. She directs it to parents, but I think most applies to us making our own spaces as well. She begins, "This human way of learning in three dimensions is a wonderful asset for sharing the faith with children with disabilities, impairments, and neurodivergences. Unlike the speech or reading or heavily language-based ways of teaching that fail to engage the attention or enable the interaction of children with disabilities, this prayer corner is a meaningful way to build the practice of hoping in God."[17] Then she gives a number of ideas for making it. First, the prayer wall, altar or corner should be the focal part of the room. Second, place different things to pray with in the space: this might include statues, prayer cards, icons, candles, buttons that repeat prayers, fake flowers, and so forth. Third, make sure some of these are within reach (if making this for an autistic child, make sure what they are most interested in is close). Finally, use all our senses to pray.

Mental Prayer

Obviously, all prayer should involve raising the mind to God. However, "mental prayer" refers specifically to a prayer that is not following a specific pre-set formula. This can be as short as pausing

---

17 Summer Kinard, "Accessible Prayer Corner Tutorial," Summer Kinard, March 28, 2019, https://summerkinard.com/2019/03/28/accessible-prayer-corner-tutorial/. (Note: Summer Kinard is Orthodox, so the focus is on icons, not statues—I make it either/or here.)

for fifteen seconds when starting a mystery of the Rosary to bring that mystery to mind, or it can be as long as spending days at a time on retreat. The next chapter will be extensively on mental prayer, but I think some notes can be made on types of mental prayer after one has learned the stages of what to do when dedicating time to this.

There are various related methods for a structure to mental prayer including *Lectio Divina*, Ignatian Contemplation, the method of Saint Sulpice, and Father John Bartunek's method.[18] We autistics can read up on and apply any of them more specifically. Here I present a six-step method that I have devised.

1. Concentrate: The first step of prayer is to enter God's presence. I need to remember that now I'm going to converse with God. That means leaving many other things to the side right now. Often an act of humility followed by a short prayer asking for and expressing faith, hope and love (the three theological virtues) can help. Specific vocal prayers can be used here, or I can offer my prayer up for some intention. Some methods suggest specific vocal prayers. This is often thought of as the preparation to enter prayer more deeply. In an analogy to human communication, it is much like small talk where you meet a friend and ask

---

18 These methods can be found in many sources. Some from whom I take elements are: John Bartunek, *The Better Part: A Christ-Centered Resource for Personal Prayer* (Algonquin, IL: Ministry23, LLC, 2011), pt. I; Adolphe Tanquerey, *The Spiritual Life: A Treatise On Ascetical And Mystical Theology*, trans. Herman Branderis, 2nd edition (Rockford, Ill.: Tan Books & Pub, 2001), 330–39; Reginald Garrigou-Lagrange, *The Three Ages of the Interior Life : Prelude of Eternal Life*, trans. Timothea Doyle, vol. 1 (Rockford, IL: TAN, 1989), 446–53.

about the weather or how their family is doing, to get your bearings. I think just as we often speed through small talk in real life, we can speed through this. Nonetheless, we can create a routine here that helps us enter God's presence. For example, we turn off our phone, sit in a particular chair, pray certain prayers from a prayer book, then dive in.

2. Capture: In this stage I grasp the material which I will be praying about during the meditation. I pick up the Bible or a spiritual book and read a section. If reading a Bible passage or a short daily reflection, like those in the second half of this book, it is often good to read through the section, then go back over it slowly.

3. Consider: Now I move from simply reading a text to entering into it. In Ignatian methods, I am invited to use my five senses to fully embrace a scene. If I am meditating on John 21 where the Risen Lord appears on the seashore, I first contemplate the sound of the waves lapping up on shore, the smell of the roasting bread and fish (the taste of them later in the story), then I hear the voice of Jesus as I feel the apostles' nets in my hands. I can reflect on a truth of the faith described in the passage. For example, take 1 John 4:16: "God is love, and he who abides in love abides in God, and God abides in him." What is meant by love here; what are the different meanings of love; have I heard someone preach on the word "agape," which is a self-giving love rather than a romantic or friendly love? Then, I consider what is meant by God being love itself and how that love is within me.

4. Converse: At this point, I start a real dialogue with Jesus to connect my meditation to my life. If I am reflecting on John 21, I might ask Jesus how I can respond more like the apostles. Maybe there is something Jesus is asking of me that is analogous to the disciples making that one last cast. If I am reflecting on how God is love, I might move to him dwelling in me and thank him for being so close to me. This is meant to be a rather informal conversation with our Lord.

5. Commit: Now I make some small resolution from what I prayed about and offer it to Jesus. Most days this is something very small about how I will live like Jesus. In the John 21 example, I might resolve to do something tough that I've been putting off or I might resolve to listen more to family members. In the 1 John 4 example, the resolution might be to express Jesus' love to a person I will see who annoys me, or to have an internal attitude to be more aware of God's presence throughout the day. The goal is not to solve everything each day, but my prayer should lead me to move forward in my imitation of Jesus: for example, to focus better in prayer if I have been distracted. Some methods talk about making an examen at this point in the meditation; others put it after contemplation, which is fine.

6. Contemplate: Although prayer should lead me to imitate Jesus in this life, the ultimate goal is preparing for the most wonderful life to come at the resurrection. It is well to spend a good amount of time just being in God's presence. This is not a time for thinking about a particular passage or asking God for anything, but just being there with him.

Often in prayer, I will go back and forth through steps three to six during a single prayer time. If a passage seems to be running dry, going back to step two might help. I've noticed that in my own daily hour of mental prayer I often do steps two through six with two different passages or meditations. This is perfectly fine. The steps are there to help us, not to mandate a strict rule that must be followed rigorously. With practice, they tend to simplify and become more fluid.[19]

Now, I think we autistics might carry out this process a little differently than neurotypicals often do. We tend to focus more on information and less on emotion. For example, if I reflect on a Gospel passage, I will almost always want to check the footnotes in my study Bible.

We tend to move from a bunch of specific points to a general principle rather than vice-versa, while neurotypicals tend to go the other way. If I want to imagine the scene or contemplate the Lord's words, I want to know all the details. As autistics we tend to remember a lot of details and make interesting connections. A detail-focus can often recognize patterns: this can easily be applied to points in the Bible or spiritual books to help our prayer.

In mental prayer, the biggest obstacle is distraction. Everyone struggles with it. Distractions are an unavoidable part of being human. Distractions mean that we are human, not that we are unholy. I think in our very categorical yes-and-no thinking, we can tend to feel that because we have distractions, we are a failure. We aren't failures at prayer, even though we sometimes fall into distractions. In fact, Father Faber, a spiritual author, notes, "No man short of a contemplative will ever reign like a despot over his vast hordes of distractions. He is a happy man, and has done much, who sets up a constitutional monarchy among them."[20]

19 For a summarized outline of this method of mental prayer, see Appendix C, page 205.

20 Frederick Faber, *Growth in Holiness or The Progress of the Spiritual Life*, 15th American edition (text from: John Murphy & Co., Baltimore, MD, 1890) (Rockford, IL: TAN, 1990), 349.

Distractions are but the surface of the soul. They may be like the waves on the surface of the water. But what matters is our focus on God in the calm depths of our soul. Most spiritual masters indicate that if we get distracted we should just turn back and refocus on prayer, not get overly concerned. Sometimes we need to realize that, despite our differences, we are still human in this way. We will get distracted at times and just need to refocus without getting overwhelmed.

Finally, I would note that in mental prayer there may be times when we are simply in a place of presence or calm. I know that sometimes during most of my hour of daily prayer, I can just look into the eyes of my images of Jesus and Mary that I mentioned above. Yet there may be days when I will read twenty-five pages of a spiritual book and not sense strongly that I spent the time with God. We must realize that the spiritual life will have these kinds of ebbs and flows. Our responsibility as Christians is to keep moving forward.

CHAPTER TWO

Deeper Prayer for the Autistic Christian

WHAT IS HAPPINESS? Some reduce it to a simple positive emotion of the moment, but it goes much deeper. Possessing or experiencing some good gives us a degree of contentment. I feel happy satisfaction holding an ice cream and consuming it, for example. But the more profound the good, the more satisfaction one feels. For example, although my dad would enjoy an ice cream, it would seem odd if he were completely overwhelmed and crying for joy like the way he was at my sister's wedding. The satisfaction of seeing your daughter marry an honorable man is a far greater good than an ice cream. Ultimately, the deepest reality we can have is our relationship with Jesus. In fact, the wisest Christian theologians like Aquinas and Augustine generally speak of the possession of this happiness as the highest good.

How do we experience God? God loves us as autistics and asks us to respond with our whole autistic selves—that is, autistically.

From a simple Our Father to the depths of mysticism our prayer will be autistic.

The question becomes: What is different between autistic prayer and neurotypical prayer? I think we can call this difference the autistic prayer-ridge,[21] as I think we autistics tend to have more struggles at the beginning yet have certain advantages once we get past those. This chapter goes deeper into the spiritual life. I hope it is all comprehensible, but some may want to accompany it with a systematic work on the spiritual life,[22] which can be read cover-to-cover or used to look up difficulties.

Difficulties Going Deeper in Prayer

Two main difficulties present themselves early in autistic prayer: theory of mind and overly emotional explanations. The first is unavoidable, the second can be lessened with effort.

When we speak of *theory of mind,* we are referring to how we form an idea of what we or others are thinking or feeling. Neurotypicals tend to do this much more subconsciously, while we autistics often struggle, since we do this much more consciously and are often not nearly as good at it. Theory of mind is important

---

21 I give a talk related to the content of this chapter on YouTube on my channel *Autistic Priest* called "The Autism Prayer Hump." It can be found at: https://youtu.be/HypFRsZ0jGo.

22 Two possible options are highly recommended: *The Spiritual Life: A Treatise on Ascetical and Mystical Theology* by Adolphe Tanqueray, SS, or *The Three Ages of the Interior Life: Preludes to Eternal Life* by Reginald Garrigou-Lagrange, O.P. Also recommended are the books by Father Thomas H. Green, S.J., which are more basic: *Opening to God: A Guide to Prayer*, and *Experiencing God: The Three Stages of Prayer*.

early in prayer as it allows the person to contemplate God's mind. It becomes even more challenging as we strive to pray with our mind and heart, not just saying words. We need to consciously work out what God could be thinking or feeling in relationship to our various acts.

We need to remember that he is a merciful and all-loving God, not simply a moral principle. We can tend to reduce him to that and thus develop an overly harsh morality. Even after years, I still struggle with seeing how much God is looking down with love when I am returning to grace in confession: I can focus too much on him as a judge of sin. This is a real issue. Even Temple Grandin, one of the most famous autistics in the United States, said she believed in God more as a principle and moral code than as a person.[23]

On top of remembering that God loves us beyond anything we can imagine, it is important to remember how we are united to him by Baptism. He has given us the theological virtues of faith, hope and love to unite ourselves with him.

We also need to realize that our relationship may be more intellectual and less emotional than we will often read in prayer books. In fact, Temple Grandin notes elsewhere, "For many people with autism, religion is intellectual rather than emotional activity."[24] An intellectual activity is just as much a human activity as

---

23 Cf. Temple Grandin, *The Way I See It: A Personal Look at Autism & Asperger's* (Arlington, TX: Future Horizons, 2015), 196–98. Grandin has addressed this topic multiple times in different works and conferences, any of which could be cited.

24 Temple Grandin, *Thinking in Pictures: My Life with Autism*, Expanded Edition (New York: Vintage, 2006), 223.

an emotional activity is. It is not even that our prayer is emotion-less, just more focused on the intellect and less on the emotion.

Autistics also struggle with the type of explanations often given in religious contexts, especially in youth groups. A neuro-typical person will generally accept an emotional explanation or stop asking why more easily. Autistics tend to keep asking why and want a logical explanation.

As an example of what I'm referring to, a teenager might ask, "Why do we have to go to Mass every Sunday?" A mom might say, "Because Jesus/the Church says so," which satisfies many. Some may ask why again and then mom responds, "It's the third command-ment," which satisfies more teens. Some may ask again, and then mom replies, "Just like you want to visit regularly with your best friend, you visit with Jesus regularly on Sunday." Some may then ask why they should have a relationship with Jesus, at which point mom may go into a discourse on how the Divine is the ultimate source of meaning and happiness along the lines of the opening paragraph to this chapter. Different autistics and neurotypicals will end up at dif-ferent degrees of asking why, but I think as an overall average, autistics will stop further down the rabbit hole.

Moreover, we autistics—and often non-autistics—can see straight through the circular logic often employed by some per-sons trying to teach catechism: "We believe in God because the Bible and catechism say so and we believe in the Bible and cate-chism because God says so." Generally this isn't laid out so clearly, but it is unfortunately all too common as an underlying presup-position in our religious education.

When people are looking for books for Catholic teens, there is often a greater emphasis on emotions than when looking for books for Catholic adults. In my teens, as an autistic young man, I went in the other direction, finding Kreeft and Tacelli's *Handbook of Christian Apologetics*[25] to be the most helpful book. After an introductory chapter, Kreeft and Tacelli offer twenty rational proofs for God's existence.

In the Church, and especially in youth groups, we tend towards emotional—and at times melodramatic—explanations that often alienate autistic young people. We take the good desire of wanting young people to have an emotional religious experience of the holy, and we focus on that as the motive of religion without realizing that other factors might be more effective.[26]

We need to help autistic young people with rational explanations of the faith or seek these out if we are autistics learning the faith. In this, it is important to use a lot of inductive reasoning, not just deductive. While most neurotypicals tend to go from the general concept to the particular, most autistics tend to go in the other direction.

Valerie Boles noted something about autistic wonder that is applicable here. She observed that autistic children tended to ask fewer questions about faith, but that when they did ask, the questions were much more often of a personal nature. She explains,

> Parents of typically developing children reported that their children's questions were more theological in nature. Children asked about creation and suffering and many other topics, some of them controversial topics frequently in the news (which was

---

25 Peter Kreeft and Ronald K. Tacelli, *Handbook of Christian Apologetics*, Reprint edition (Downers Grove, Ill: IVP Academic, 1994).

26 See Paul Dearey, "Do the Autistic Have a Prayer?," *Journal of Religion, Disability & Health* 13, no. 1 (February 3, 2009): 42–43, https://doi.org/10.1080/15228960802581420.

absent in the population of children with autism). About 50 percent of the questions children with autism asked were more personal. . . . All of the questions asked by children with autism were about their own sufferings (a classmate's death) or perceived shortcomings in religion.[27]

Later, Boles makes this even more explicit, "Children with autism spectrum disorder were four times as likely to ask questions related to their own personal spiritual experience than those who were typically developing."[28] These questions indicate our own struggles that need good answers.

Prayer in the Fast Lane

Once we autistics get over those initial difficulties, I think we have a few traits that can accelerate our growth in prayer. Let's examine, first of all, wordless communication. Communicating with God does not need words. Communicating with other humans requires audible words. There is a whole process for most communication that we struggle with, but it isn't needed to communicate with God. To communicate between humans, we need to transfer our thoughts into words, say those words, the other needs to hear the sounds, make out the words, and then understand them according to their thoughts. And then when the

---

27 Valerie Boles, "Understanding the Religious Experience of Children with Autism in the Catholic Church: An Overview of Contextual and Behavioral Factors" (Saint Francis University, 2019), 16–17, https://www.semanticscholar.org/paper/Running-head%3A-RELIGION-AND-AUTISM-1-Understanding-Boles/37313ec05b056ae25e8b640a6f68f979aa3384a4.

28 Ibid., 20.

communication comes back, the same process needs to be repeated the other way.

Most humans do this automatically and assume that the other's thoughts are the same as their own. This doesn't always work out, even for neurotypicals. This process is particularly challenging for many autistics, especially when emotions are involved: we can have trouble even identifying our own emotions clearly. Some autistics even have alexithymia, or the inability to be aware of their own feelings. I feel a kind of malaise and dissatisfaction, but is it sadness or anger or stress or anxiety or . . . I don't know.

Since God is, as Augustine says, "more inward to me than my most inward part; and higher than my highest,"[29] he knows our thoughts and feelings. As he is inward and relies not on outward communication, he can also communicate his thoughts directly to us without the mediation of human language.

I don't know if telepathic communication exists between humans, but I know it exists between God and man. As God can read my mind, my prayer can stay in wordless concepts and images without ever having to worry about speaking and listening, as we communicate both ways in pure thought. The thoughts I have in prayer and the thoughts God transfers to me are often difficult to put into words.

Saint John of the Cross describes a similar lack of words—and at times even images—as we approach divine union. He describes

---

29 Augustine of Hippo, "Confessions," in *Nicene and Post-Nicene Fathers, First Series*, trans. J. G. Pilkington, vol. 1 (Buffalo, NY: Christian Literature, 1887), bk. III, chap. 6, par. 11, https://www.newadvent.org/fathers/110103.htm.

how the images from our senses slowly fade away as we move toward divine union. God is so far beyond sensory images that the images fail to grasp how wonderful union with him is.[30]

We autistics often struggle to translate into words and sounds what is in our mind. We often need to put far more conscious energy into that process. But because of that, we are more adapted for a situation where the process is no longer needed, such as when we reach a certain level of communication mind-to-mind with God. So once over the ridge, we can accelerate down the slope, as we aren't held back by such a process. I think we can adapt to this "telepathic" communication quicker and more easily. We can find it easier to communicate with God than with our fellow humans.

Related to this is the autistic ability to focus. Kelly,[31] an autistic young lady, noted, "I feel in a way that I've got more of an advantage with my prayer life than a neurotypical, as I can just sort of switch off from the world around me and engage my thoughts with God."

Second, as we advance in prayer, senses become less important. A large part of autism is that the filters between our senses and our conscious brain are different from the standard ones that neurotypicals have. This is what causes all our sensory issues. As pointed

---

30 See John of the Cross, *The Ascent of Mount Carmel*, ed. Benedict Zimmerman, trans. David Lewis (London: T. Baker, 1906), 112 (Bk. II, Chap. XII, par. 5), http://archive.org/details/TheAscentOfMountCarmel.

31 I communicated with a number of autistic individuals in preparing this book to get a wider perspective of different autistic prayer experiences. I asked them all permission to use their content but promised them anonymity. Kelly is a pseudonym and whenever an autistic individual appears without a last name or footnote, the name is a pseudonym for one of these anonymous testimonies and the quotations are what he or she told me.

out in the reference to Saint John of the Cross above, deep union with God is beyond the senses. As senses become less important, as we approach the deeper spiritual union that all the spiritual masters speak of, we can concern ourselves less with sense interpretation. Thus, we need not be preoccupied by these sensory issues.

Third, the autistic logical foundation tends to be more solid than the more emotional foundation neurotypicals may have for their spiritual life. We autistics often need a reason: if you say I should do X because you say so, I will pretty much ignore you. If you give me a decent reason, I will generally follow through. We need a reason why, but once we have that reason, we remain steadfast in our resolve.

If we understand the logical reasons for God's existence and then logical reasons to worship him on Sunday, we can easily be steadfast. We just need to learn this logically. Personally, philosophy has always interested me, as it gave the ultimate answers in logical form. Some claim to be atheistic philosophers, but if you properly understand philosophy, you will clearly see the logic that God exists. Often people give Aquinas' five proofs for the existence of God, which are good; however, they are not the only proofs.[32]

Fourth, since we autistics tend to make such strong logical connections, we are often quite good at seeing God in nature. When on retreat, I like to walk in the park or the woods as the very existence of the trees and birds reminds me of how God takes care of me. Thus, the rejection or absence of natural theology in a lot of modern religious instruction is problematic. (Natural theology is a

---

32 Cf. Kreeft and Tacelli, *Handbook*, pt. 2: God, pp. 45–101.

branch of philosophy that treats what we can know about God from the world and reason—both of which tend to be autistic strengths.)

This sense of seeing God in nature reminds us also of autistics' tendency toward wonder. Our way of seeing all the particulars means that things in nature or in prayer can bring us a sense of awe and wonder more easily. I look at a sunset or a waterfall and am taken aback by the thought of how great is the God who made this wonderful thing. It is amazing to me.

Finally, a great advantage we autistics have is our great long-term memory. As I mentioned earlier, in the seminary I got the nickname Schneider-pedia because I seemed to remember every fact. This was not despite my autism but because of it. In my prayer and in listening to others preach, I can recall lots of information from the Bible or spiritual authors with little effort. I have never dedicated time to memorizing most of this information. When we did have to memorize something in the seminary, my short-term memory was slightly above average but by no means great, while my long-term memory of facts is off the charts as far as I can tell. Different descriptions show that many autistics are like this. This memory can connect all the different aspects of prayer.

Autism at the Deepest Levels of Prayer

Often humans tend to reduce prayer to prayers of petition. A person prays for his or her spouse or sick grandma. However, this is far from the deepest level of prayer. The deepest level of prayer is a personal encounter with God in the depths of the soul. I think three aspects are important as the autistic seeks to reach deeper levels of prayer.

First, we know that God loves us for who we are and communicates according to the way we receive his message. We know that God speaks to people whether they speak Chinese or English. We know that God speaks often in signs that might not otherwise be obvious: for example, God may speak to me through the pitter-patter of the rain or through an inspiration in my mind that I could easily miss if inattentive. We know that many describe it as "beyond words," and we know that God is so wonderful that he really is beyond words. Saint Paul noted in 1 Corinthians 9:22, "I have become all things to all men, that I might by all means save some." Thus, we can expect him to communicate to me as an autistic person autistically, in a manner appropriate for my autism—even though God is not autistic any more than he is American when he communicates in English.

We reason to this knowing the nature of God and knowing, too, that the nature of love is to make oneself like the other and to love in a way to which the other is receptive. Moreover, I can also say from experience that in deep prayer, I don't need to think about the social clues, the translation from autistic English to standard English, or even—at times—the translation of ideas to words. I communicate to God autistically and he communicates back on a deeper level than any word can hope to describe.

Also important to our search for deeper prayer is the structure of mental prayer as explained in a previous chapter. Mental prayer involves putting yourself in a Bible scene or imagining some moment like the earth's creation or the last judgment. Many autistics have great imaginations and very keen senses, so we can bring these to life beyond words. I have extreme visualizations of many different Bible passages and Christian truths that are far beyond words. I zoom in on one microscopic thing, then immediately I'm overhead watching in slow motion, then I zoom in on some other aspect. I will bring out a few of these in the different devotions in this book.

Finally, the deepest prayer of union and contemplation reaches something else entirely. This is our whole self completely open to God and infused with his spirit. We should all open ourselves to the point that we can receive divine contemplation, even though some authors debate if all are called to it. Some experience contemplation in a consistent way, but many others experience it in a series of flashes. The nature of such infused contemplation is beyond what I want to talk about now. Although infused contemplation is a gift, ordinarily several things are needed before this gift is given. In some ways, I think we autistics start further along the path to where it may be given than others. We need profound openness to God and profound humility. Autistics tend to be very open with those they know and trust. We can even "over-share" about ourselves more easily than being too reserved. Regarding humility, our rationality tends to think more of goals and the good of all, not so much personal gain. We are naturally less concerned about others' opinions and less pretentious. We can see this in how trusting we are of others and how we tend to be so morally upright that people might consider us scrupulous. On his blog, AspiePriest noted that during his formation he was thought to be dishonest about his past, since he had done so little wrong.[33] I never encountered that, but I can see how we autistics could be so labeled.

Religion often focuses on aesthetic aspects like art, music, architecture, etc., that help us enter into the liturgy or other

---

[33] See aspiepriest, "MMPI-2," *Aspiepriest* (blog), June 24, 2016, https://aspiepriest.wordpress.com/tag/mmpi-2/.

prayers. However, these are for the initial stages and fade as we approach deeper union. In an academic analysis of autistic prayer, Paul Dearey noted, "Such aesthetic solutions do nothing to reflect the adoration that is due to the God who reveals the mystery of his divinity."[34] Divinity is so far beyond any image we could have of it.

One autistic young woman, Samantha, described her prayer: "NTs [Neurotypicals] seem to be emotionally involved with prayer; it seems to be about how praying makes you feel (or, in some cases, look). The only thing I need to feel to know that I am praying is a lack of emotion, a stillness, a surrendering of my conscious self. NTs seem to be caught up in the idea of having the right words, praying for the right things. I do not feel the need for words so much as concepts and openness."

Once we begin praying consistently, I think we autistics might be set to move easily to deeper levels of prayer. We will often be able to move past discursive prayer when there are signs to transition to contemplation. We have amazing imagination, and we are naturally humble and open with God. We can communicate with God in our way and he will respond in turn.

Autistic Missionaries to an Autistic World

Finally, we autistics should not simply pray: we should go forward and spread the message of Jesus to our fellow autistics. We Christians are called to go and make disciples of every nation, every people, and every culture (cf. Mt 28:19). We can easily think of this primarily as missions to other countries, but it also includes

---

34 Dearey, "Do the Autistic Have a Prayer?" 46.

missions to people in our countries who communicate differently, such as autistics. This realization came to me during a Canon Law class of all places. Dr. Ed Peters, who has a deaf son, spoke of how the Deaf have a different culture, since they communicate differently, using American Sign Language. Hence, we need missionaries from the hearing world, but also Deaf missionaries to evangelize that world. He explained how the grammar is different[35] and how signs relate to each other differently than do words in English. As an example, we might note that "sign" and "sing" are written similarly, while an ASL signer might notice that "Russia" and "brag" are similar, as they both involve hands on hips.[36]

Likewise, I think that we as autistics have a different culture because we have a different language. On the surface it is modern English, but as we get to certain elements of the language, that similarity fades. Body language is a large part of standard non-written English; however, it's very different in autistic English. In standard English, people tease each other, yet when autistics try this, it comes off as insulting. In autistic English, small talk and emotional words almost vanish from the vocabulary. Furthermore, how language functions in our mind is different. Language relies on a connection between a word, a thought, and a thing. For example, when someone points and says, "dog," some idea of "dogness" exists in their mind and there is a particular

---

35 Cf. Rochelle Barlow, "Sign Language Sentences: The Basic Structure," ASL Rochelle, 2019, 2013, https://aslrochelle.com/blog/sign-language-sentences-the-basic-structure.

36 Cf. Brenda Cartwrght, "Signs That Are Close . . . But Not the Same: Set 1 | Signing Savvy Articles," Signing Savvy, April 8, 2016, https://www.signingsavvy.com/blog/173/Signs+That+Are+Close . . . +But+Not+the+Same+-+Set+1.

dog over there which matches that idea. Normal English tends to be more flexible and abstract while the autistic language is more concrete. For most neurotypicals, "dogness" refers to some kind of abstract idea of what a dog is, maybe a definition like "furry four-legged carnivore with a wet nose that is a pet." But for autistics, the "dogness" first in our mind is visualizing a dozen different dogs we remember. Although some of us will get quite skilled at speaking normal English, it will always be a bit of a second language. (A second language does not mean we cannot be fluent in standard English, but that it is not the natural way we would speak and takes more effort. I can preach and hear confession in Spanish but, being a second-language confessor, I need to take more frequent breaks if the confession line is long, since speaking requires more effort.)

Initial efforts have been made to recognize the autistic community as having special needs. All of these efforts are missionary work from outside the community, not looking at things from an autistic perspective. For example, a Catholic publisher developed kits to help make sacramental preparation more accessible.[37] These were prepared by the brother and parents of an autistic young woman, not by an autistic individual. These seem to be more about intellectual difficulties than strictly about autism. I personally went through the normal route and had no serious difficulties. A few books have been written for parishes or churches to welcome autistic members. These seem good in the types of things they suggest—and I will even steal a few ideas from them—but they are

---

37 Cf. "Adaptive Learning Kits," Loyola Press, 2020, https://www.loyolapress.com/faith-formation/special-needs/adaptive-learning-kits/.

from the perspective of non-autistic members welcoming the autistic members of the Church.

Lamar Hardwick was one of the first people to speak of Christianity from the autistic perspective. He might be seen as a first missionary to autistics from within our community. His book, *I Am Strong*, is a good story of how he became a pastor, despite the obvious challenges that autism brings to such a role. He is successful as a pastor to a local community. I want to go deeper in attempting to inculturate the Gospel for autistics.

Aimée O'Connell and Father Mark P. Nolette have created an online community with *Autism Consecrated: The Mission of St. Thorlák*.[38] They have worked on various resources from autistic Stations of the Cross to an autistic reading of the *Baltimore Catechism*, as well as resources for parishes to include autistics. They also tried to arrange an in-person meeting to discuss autism and Catholicism, but the first attempt was cancelled due to the COVID-19 pandemic. (Writing this here is kind of paradoxical because I wrote the first draft of this chapter as a talk for this conference.) It is interesting to note that Aimée takes Saint Thorlák, an Icelandic bishop, to likely be autistic and has written a biography of him,[39] which can be helpful in viewing an autistic saint as a role model.

Inculturation is not a term you might be used to, but in the mission work of the Church it is important. The Gospel is

---

38 https://autismconsecrated.com/.

39 Aimée O'Connell and John C. Wilhelmsson, *Thorlák of Iceland: Who Rose Above Autism to Become Patron Saint of His People* (San Jose, CA: Chaos to Order Publishing, 2018).

universal but ways of celebrating it vary from place to place. For example, my community has a mission territory among the Maya people, the descendants of the Mayan civilization. The people had a form of ancestor worship, and so the priests had to decipher what would be a proper way for the people to honor their ancestors while making it clear that they no longer worshiped them. If I go to an average English-speaking Catholic parish in the USA and then go to the plaza before Our Lady of Guadalupe in Mexico City, I will see people expressing their faith in different ways while maintaining the same faith. Inculturation brings the faith into a certain cultural or social reality. It is not about modifying or watering down the faith but re-presenting it anew to a different culture.

I am sure we haven't discovered all the ways to inculturate the faith to an autistic audience. Books like this one and Dr. Hardwick's are—in a way—a first attempt at inculturating the faith to autistics. I don't expect to be perfect, but I do intend to keep some important truths in mind: the orthodoxy of the Catholic faith and the reality of being autistic. I hope, with those two poles, I won't go astray.

There have been many suggestions on how the Church needs to include the disabled to fulfill its mission. I will note two of these, then look at how they apply to us autistics.

An assembly of the World Council of Churches noted,

> The Church cannot exemplify 'the full humanity revealed in Christ,' bear witness to the interdependence of humankind, or achieve unity in diversity if it continues to acquiesce in the social isolation of disabled persons and to deny them full participation in its life. The unity of the family of God is handicapped where these brothers and sisters are treated as objects of condescending charity. It is broken where they are left

out. . . . How can the Church be open to the witness which Christ extends through them?[40]

This is not a sense of dividing humankind into groups, but some of us need to receive certain accommodations in order to participate.

We can also note what Bob Quinlan from the National Catholic Partnership on Disability told me: "I'm not just trying to help them out on a one-way channel that comes back and helps me; I want to help them become good, to help them to give back as they can."[41] This reminds us that we autistics are called to evangelize. We are the voice God asks to speak to others whose native language is also autistic English.

As autistics, we are often excluded from Church due to social barriers. A lot of us are less committed to religion than Americans in general. This leaves evangelizing autistic people as an open mission field. We need to work both on ways we can grow spiritually on our own—as this book attempts—and look at better ways of integrating in the wider Church.

Let's conclude this section with Pope Francis' words about the disabled in December 2019. He first notes that everyone needs to

---

40 Fifth Assembly of the WCC, Nairobi, 1975, "Report of Section II: What Unity Requires," in *The Ecumenical Movement: An Anthology of Key Texts and Voices*, ed. Michael Kinnamon and Brian E. Cope (Grand Rapids, MI: World Council of Churches/Conseil Oecumenique des Eglises, 1997), 112.

41 Matthew Schneider, *How to Live Catholic Social Teaching: Interviews at the Catholic Social Ministries Gathering 2016* (Washington, DC, 2016), https://www.youtube.com/watch?v=XyAWX3PrHnA&ab_channel=FrMatthewP.Schneider%2CLC.

see the disabled in their full humanity, as the presence of Christ in our brothers and sisters. Then he gets practical. To properly care for and accompany the disabled, Francis proposes that we begin "taking on situations of marginalization with strength and tenderness; making way with them and 'anointing them' with dignity for an active participation in the civil and ecclesial community." He wants not only barriers to change but mentalities to change: "Making good laws and breaking down physical barriers is important, but it is not enough, if the mentality does not change as well, if we do not overcome a widespread culture that continues to produce inequalities, preventing people with disabilities from actively participating in ordinary life."[42] This leads us to help all the disabled become ministers, not just ministered to. This includes us autistics.

---

42 Pope Francis, "Message to Mark the International Day of Persons with Disabilities" (Vatican, December 3, 2019), http://www.vatican.va/content/francesco/en/messages/pont-messages/2019/documents/papa-francesco_20191203_messaggio-disabilita.html. I did a longer analysis of this speech in my blog: Matthew Schneider, "Pope Francis: The Disabled Can Be Ministers, Not Just Ministered To," *Through Catholic Lenses* (blog), December 4, 2019, https://www.patheos.com/blogs/throughcatholiclenses/2019/12/pope-francis-recognize-accompany-the-disabled/.

CHAPTER THREE

Myths about Autism and Prayer

WHEN I OPEN YouTube and search "autism prayer" or "autistic prayer," some of my videos come up at the bottom of the first page. However, they are drowned out by other videos.

One older but popular video is a family prayer for those with autistic children. The prayer has a long petition: "Heavenly Father . . . give these parents wisdom and angelic help in their care for their children, help the child's siblings to be patient and to grow in self-giving love, grant these families our special support and give them friends who understand and love them."[43] You might notice that the prayer is not directed to helping the autistic child at all, nor does it suggest that the autistic child pray the prayer: it only asks help for those family members around the child. It doesn't ask the autistic person to pray that God will lead

---

43 *Prayer for Those with Autistic Children* (EWTN, 2011), https://www.youtube.com/watch?v=EHxcHeWTorA&ab_channel=EWTN.

him or her in right paths or something similar. This might be an oversight, but other videos are worse.

The pastor of a Maryland church has a video of him praying out the spirit of autism. He concludes, "I command your daughter to be set lose from every demonic oppression, of any autism spirit, in Jesus' name."[44] This person is not alone. Another YouTube channel has a person praying while the prayer text appears on screen. One screen of text says things like: "I bind the spirit of autism," and "You are healed and delivered of autism."[45] An Australian pastor states, "God, I break autism right now. . . . We thank you God for your anointing power that's flowing right now and breaking autism."[46] Compared to other videos on the topic, these four are some of the most viewed videos. Some of the other top videos have had issues too. Another faith healer, named Becky Dvorak, who I came across elsewhere, said, "Autism is from Satan. It's demons."[47] Becky claims that her adopted child used to be autistic, but is no longer so.

---

[44] *Prayer Against Autism: "Prayer for Autistic Children," "Deliverance Prayers for Kid with Autism"* (Kay ElBlessing, 2014), https://www.youtube.com/watch?v=3e9_E9ehbSE&ab_channel=KayElBlessing.

[45] *Prayer for Autism: Journey to Breakthrough* (Rosetta Daniels, 2016), https://www.youtube.com/watch?v=qVZHxunhnVg&ab_channel=RosettaDaniels.

[46] *Prayer for Healing of Autism—John Mellor Ministry of Healing & Miracles* (John Mellor, 2014), https://www.youtube.com/watch?v=XoyT6PTAljY&ab_channel =JohnMellor.

[47] *Autism Healing and Deliverance Seminar* (Becky Dvorak Healing And Miracles, 2017), https://www.youtube.com/watch?v=qpUfZcOoc1g.

Autism is a variation in brain structure, not a demonic influence. It is not a spirit to be broken. It is not that a child is oppressed by darkness. Autism is something that stays with us lifelong, even though we can adapt to the non-autistic world in varying degrees throughout our life. With help and prayer, a child might reach the point where he or she can get an A-average in a mainstream school classroom, but that doesn't mean that the child is not autistic. It means that he or she has a found a way to succeed as an autistic student.

This kind of idea that we need to pray the autism out is the first myth. The myths that autistics can't pray and that we intrinsically have preternatural gifts will be addressed further on.

We Don't Need the Autism "Prayed Out"

The idea that autism can be prayed out seems to come in two forms. The first form is a sense that autism is demonic; the second form admits that autism is a physical disorder but over-spiritualizes it, blaming it on particular sins. I will use quotes from Torben Søndergaard and Father Dominic Valanmanal as examples. I will refute both and then point out additional reasons not to presume to pray autism away.

Torben Søndergaard is the founder of *The Last Reformation*. He focuses on faith healing, including healing from autism. He has been given positive press on major Christian programs like CBN's *The 700 Club*.

After a trip to Australia Torben posted a video saying, "We see many people set free from demons and healed and one of them was a young girl nine years old who had autism, and that young girl with autism and a lot of other problems . . . one night in the meeting, my friend Michael just prayed for her and that spirit just left her."[48] Another time Torben said: "Do I believe autism could be demonic or influenced by something and people can get healed of it? Of course, I do. I believe people can get healed of every kind of sickness; I believe in a God who created heaven and earth; I believe God can heal everyone."[49]

Rebecca Giles, a young autistic woman who was involved with this group and other similar groups like Becky Dvorak's, described her experience with these groups.

> I remember the stinging comments that Christians have said to me: "Nobody knows what causes autism, but it seems obvious that demons are involved somehow." "I'm not sure how much demons are involved with autism." "Demons cause autism."
>
> Every one of these people meant well, but their words were destructive instead. You can't suggest to an autistic person (or to the parents of an autistic child) that demons may cause autism without causing great harm and distress by your words.[50]

Giles describes how people attempted to pray out her autism. One even made her very uncomfortable by grasping her neck during an attempted exorcism. Another time, a woman said she saw bats flying around Rebecca's head. This made her feel rejected; it

---

[48] Torben Søndergaard, *Torben Søndergaard on Facebook Watch* (Torben Søndergaard, 2016), https://www.facebook.com/watch/?t=12&v=161526937551710.

[49] Torben Søndergaard 51:55 of https://www.youtube.com/watch?v=Z9uFHcovw8o&t=2982s&ab_channel=TheLastReformation

[50] Rebecca Giles, "Is Autism Demonic?," Christian Autistic, April 17, 2020, https://rebeccagilesart.wixsite.com/christianautistic/post/is-autism-demonic.

made her feel as if from their perspective she was choosing the demons over Jesus. But at the same time, Rebecca knew she hadn't chosen to be autistic. Ultimately, she indicates, "I felt as if my autism was a barrier between me and God, as if I must make a choice between being Christian or being autistic."[51] That is a horrendous position in which to place a young Christian.

Instead, as Christians, we are called to trust faith and reason, not just faith. We check for mental health causes first before making any determination that certain behaviors might be caused by demons. A deacon-psychologist who did such tests for a diocese before a priest did an exorcism noted that many individuals clearly had mental issues, but others exhibited disturbing symptoms that could indicate demonic influence. Nevertheless, autism is clearly biological: let's not attribute to demons what seems evidently due to biology. Moreover, we know that God makes each of us perfect in his eyes. If we are autistic from birth, that perfection would include autism. Part of how God makes each person perfect is by giving him or her certain qualities that will become a cross to bear. Certain aspects of being autistic are clearly a cross.

Father Dominic Valanmanal is a Catholic priest from India who also has a misguided view of praying autism away. He does not believe that autism is caused directly by demons, but takes the view that the cause is familial sin. He said in a sermon,

> Why does this generation have autism and hyperactivity? . . . Adultery, masturbation, homosexuality, porn, if you are addicted to these, I say to you in the name of God . . . when you

---

51 Ibid.

get married and have children, there is a high possibility of bearing these types of children. They lead an animal-like life. They copulate like animals. They bear children like animals. Therefore, those children also, will be like animals.[52]

I can tell you that my parents weren't perfect, but I see none of what he mentions in them, yet I am autistic. Then there are other parents who had all kinds of issues like those mentioned above, yet none of their children were autistic. His logic puts added negative pressure from the community on parents, making others assume that the parents were highly immoral even if they weren't.

Although the moral issues Father Dominic mentions can cause family trauma resulting in other conditions like anxiety or PTSD (Post-Traumatic Stress Disorder), those issues do not seem to have a significant effect on autism. The best estimates currently put autism at 60 to 90 percent genetic,[53] from a wide variety of genes. The main non-genetic cause seems to be the in-utero environment. The sins he mentions have little connection to that.

Fortunately, bishops in Canada and Ireland have canceled events where Father Valanmanal was to preach his message, and he himself canceled a trip to Australia when a similar result seemed

---

52 Patsy McGarry, "Invitation to Priest Who Blames Autism on Parents 'Should Be Withdrawn,'" The Irish Times, accessed May 20, 2020, https://www.irishtimes.com/news/social-affairs/religion-and-beliefs/invitation-to-priest-who-blames-autism-on-parents-should-be-withdrawn-1.3917042.

53 Cf. Joachim Hallmayer et al., "Genetic Heritability and Shared Environmental Factors Among Twin Pairs With Autism," Archives of General Psychiatry 68, no. 11 (November 2011): 1095–1102, https://doi.org/10.1001/archgenpsychiatry.2011.76.

likely.[54] But unfortunately, at his retreat center in India he still runs events where he continues to give the same message. He offered an apology for his words, but never took responsibility for them or indicated that he was changing his position. He was just sorry "it was misinterpreted and misunderstood."[55]

Jesus makes it clear that parental sin does not cause health issues. In John 9:3, he says, "It was not that this man sinned, or his parents, but that the works of God might be made manifest in him." Even though the blind man's parents may have been in sin when he was born, that sin was not the cause of his blindness. On top of that, autism is not directly an illness, but more a diverse neurotype that tends to cause difficulties.

Both of the above interpretations seem to create an attitude that belittles the autistic individual. I doubt that my autistic readers felt uplifted by either of these descriptions of autism. Autism is not easy. I would not say that living in this world is easier for autistics than neurotypicals. Describing me or my autistic friends as animals or comparing us to the demon-possessed in the Bible is completely unfair and inaccurate.

Furthermore, setting aside the above mistaken ideas, most autistics don't want to be cured. In 2018 an extensive survey asked

---

54 Cf. Matthew Schneider, "Autism Is NOT Due to Parental Sin, Fr. Valanmanal," *Through Catholic Lenses* (blog), July 23, 2019, https://www.patheos.com/blogs/throughcatholiclenses/2019/07/autism-is-not-due-to-parental-sin-fr-valanmahal/.

55 Matthew Schneider, "Fr. Dominic Valanmanal, Please Stop Attacking Autistics UPDATED," *Through Catholic Lenses* (blog), November 18, 2019, https://www.patheos.com/blogs/throughcatholiclenses/2019/11/fr-dominic-valanmanal-please-stop-attacking-autistics/.

autistics and family members of autistics if they would cure themselves or their family member if some means were available. There
were five options, ranging from strongly agree to strongly disagree.
The family members were about even, with the middle response,
neither "agree" nor "disagree," getting the highest result. On the
other hand, 52 percent of autistics themselves strongly disagreed
and another 20 percent disagreed less vehemently. Even non-verbal
autistics or those with several learning disabilities disagreed with a
cure by 75 percent and 69 percent respectively.[56] This does not
mean that we don't want help with matters like anxiety, getting
along with neurotypicals, dealing with sensory overload situations,
etc. What most of us see is that autism is part of who we are, part
of our personality: thus, curing our autism would mean that we
would become someone else. I can be less anxious and still be
myself, but I cannot be non-autistic and still be myself.

We Can Pray

While the first myth of needing to pray autism away is sometimes explicit, the next myth is often implicit. It is shown more
through absence than presence. It is seen in prayers like the one
cited above that does not include a prayer directly by or for autistic
individuals but only by and for all those around them.

Once I was diagnosed, I started looking for prayer resources
for autistics. I found several resources for parents, but most

---

[56] See "11,521 People Answered This Autism Survey. Warning: The Results
May Challenge You," Autistic Not Weird, October 1, 2018, https://
autisticnotweird.com/2018survey/.

described praying *for* the autistic child, not *with* the autistic child. A blog post here or there would have an autistic describing his or her own prayer life. But resources in general seemed to imply that we couldn't pray, or that our prayers had little value.

A Jewish therapist wrote in *Psychology Today* about her autistic son's prayer. She noted how he struggles with English, but instead seems attracted to rituals in prayer like lighting the menorah or saying prayers in Hebrew, although he doesn't understand Hebrew. She attempts to describe his prayer; however, she remains uncertain if it is actual communication with God or simply an autistic love of ritual. She hopes that as he gets older, he will be able to describe it better to her.[57] I too would be cautious about stating what others experience in prayer. Unfortunately, beyond a few posts on forums or blogs, this is one of the better published descriptions of autistic prayer.

Some even question how much of a theory of mind is needed to understand a personal God. Matthew Hutson states, "Belief in God depends on theory of mind."[58] A basic issue in autism is that we have a weak or non-existent theory of mind: we struggle to guess what another person is thinking or feeling just from his or her external actions. What others do subconsciously, we struggle with: some manage to do it passably well by using conscious

---

57 Cf. "What Does My Autistic Son Get Out of Prayer?," Psychology Today, accessed May 21, 2020, https://www.psychologytoday.com/blog/all-families-are-not-alike/201812/what-does-my-autistic-son-get-out-prayer.

58 Matthew Hutson, "Does Autism Lead to Atheism?," Psychology Today, May 30, 2012, http://www.psychologytoday.com/blog/psyched/201205/does-autism-lead-atheism.

processes, but even if we succeed, we are expending a lot more effort than neurotypicals.

Because of the dearth of material on autistic prayer, I went out of my way to interview a wide swath of autistic Christians when preparing this book. I collected a few dozen testimonies of autistic individuals who were happy to tell me about their prayer. I myself have prayed several hours a day for two decades. Jesus calls every person to pray.

Some might think of prayer as speech, and speech is often absent in autistic individuals. However, not all prayer consists of words, let alone words spoken aloud. Often such autistics can pray words silently or can pray thoughts. A lack of verbal ability should not take away the thought that this person can pray.[59]

In fact, the *Catechism* (2567) teaches that all of us, including autistics, are called to pray. It states: "The living and true God tirelessly calls each person to that mysterious encounter known as prayer. In prayer, the faithful God's initiative of love always comes first; our own first step is always a response." Throughout the book of Acts, we see all the Christians praying together, and nobody who has accepted Jesus and been baptized seems ever to be excluded.

Furthermore, all are called to be saints, whatever our psychological conditions. When writing about depression, Aaron Kheriaty and Father John Cihak note, "Throughout history, many saints and people of heroic virtue suffered from mental illness of one sort or another. If we do not recognize this fact, we run the

---

[59] See Dearey, "Do the Autistic Have a Prayer?," 42.

risk of uncharitably and unjustly stigmatizing those who suffer from depression."[60] Likewise we need to avoid stigmatizing autism and recognize that autistics are called to be and can become saints.

We Aren't Automatic Psychics

William Stillman has written three of the most popular works on the topic of autism and spirituality.[61] Stillman takes a syncretistic or New Age perspective. Not everything Stillman says is wrong, but his works contain a preponderance of error.

We know that spiritual gifts like prophecy or reading another soul exist—there are saints who had them. It also seems that these may be somewhat more evident in autistics, since we, more than neurotypicals, can tend to continue into adulthood with a childlike faith. Those with gifts but without a childlike faith would usually be less aware of the gifts and use them less, so these gifts would not be evident even if present. Here "childlike" needs to be distinguished from "childish." Childlike refers to someone who relates to God simply, a person for whom faith and the spiritual world seem ordinary in this life, whereas childish means self-centered and petty. We can take Saint Therese of Lisieux as a model

60 Aaron Kheriaty and Fr John Cihak, *Catholic Guide to Depression*, Kindle (Manchester, NH: Sophia Institute Press, 2012), Introduction.

61 William Stillman, *Autism and the God Connection*, (Naperville, IL: Sourcebooks, 2006); *The Soul of Autism: Looking Beyond Labels to Unveil Spiritual Secrets of the Heart Savants*, Kindle (Franklin Lakes, NJ: New Page Books, 2008); *The Autism Prophecies: How an Evolution of Healers and Intuitives Is Influencing Our Spiritual Future*, Kindle (Franklin Lakes, NJ: New Page Books, 2010).

of childlike faith. Stillman notes, "Children . . . , as the purest of innocents, often perceive spiritual experiences only because they haven't yet been conditioned *not to*."[62]

Stillman includes some examples of such a positive childlike faith. He quotes a dad speaking about his then three-year-old autistic son Matt leaving his Batman action figures before Mary.[63] It is great to see little kids be so aware of Jesus. However, this is a trait of some kids raised by religious parents, whether the kids are autistic or not. Stillman gets several other things right, as in one passage about the conscience; he also rightly notes how the autistic tendency to be inquisitive and curious will play out spiritually.

The problem is that Stillman will constantly mix these ideas into a syncretistic or New Age formulation that is both inaccurate in describing most autistic experience and contrary to Christian faith. His official website title, "Autism Whisperer and Psychic Visionary,"[64] leaves little doubt as to his perspective. He explains his own experience: "It was necessary for me to create my own divine byway to attain authenticity and harvest the spiritual reserve to which I was entitled."[65] Creating his own path to God is

---

62 Stillman, *Autism and the God Connection*, chap. three: "Speaking in Silence." This is also quoted positively indicating the spiritual depth from autistic simplicity in: Olga Bogdashina, *Autism and Spirituality: Psyche, Self and Spirit in People on the Autism Spectrum*, Kindle (London: Jessica Kingsley Publishers, 2013), 50–51.

63 See Stillman, *Soul of Autism*, chap. seven: "Prince of Peace."

64 Stillman, "Autism Whisperer and Psychic Visionary | William Stillman," accessed May 26, 2020, https://www.williamstillman.com/.

65 Stillman, *Soul of Autism*, chap. eight: "Pathways to Spiritual Wellness."

quite problematic for the Christian who knows that Jesus is "the way, and the truth, and the life" (Jn 14:6).

Two particularly problematic sections are about reincarnation and Reiki.[66] Stillman quotes a forty-seven-year-old autistic about his memory of past lives, "Before this incarnation I chose to be born with a disability. I wanted/needed to experience being dependent on others to live. In my other lifetimes I have ruled, led, and taught others."[67] Past lives do *not* exist. We have one life in this world and God creates our soul at our conception.

He quotes a mother named Tricia about her family's experience of Reiki, which he sees as completely positive.[68] Getting specific in his final book, Stillman endorses *A Course in Miracles*, directly endorsing one of its heresies—that the physical world is an illusion.[69]

Stillman's explanation does not match reality. He tries inadequately to respond to his critics, arguing that they don't take into account the following: "I do not presume to be writing about—or representing—*all* persons on the autism spectrum; this is why I have always been careful to use the words *many*, *most*, and *some*,

---

66 "Reiki is a Japanese spiritual practice where hands are laid close to a person but not touching them, so that, according to practitioners, the universal life force is transferred. Christian theology and all scientific evidence say that such universal energy does not exist as similar calming, non-reiki activities produce as much help for patients." M. S. Lee, M. H. Pittler, and E. Ernst. 2008: "Effects of Reiki in Clinical Practice: A Systematic Review of Randomized Clinical Trials," *International Journal of Clinical Practice* 62 (6): 947–54. https://doi.org/10.1111/j.1742-1241.2008.01729.x.

67 Stillman, *The Autism Prophecies*, chap. seven: "Casting the Net."

68 See Stillman, chap. two: "The Art of Healing."

69 See Stillman, chap. one: "The Mechanics of Miracles."

not *every* or *all*."[70] However, when he starts talking about pre-birth memories, telepathic communication, Reiki, and so forth, I really wonder if what he says can be applied to most. I am pretty connected to autistics online and those making such claims are a miniscule minority.

Furthermore, Stillman accepts some very problematic ideas about the increase in autism. He argues that the increase in diagnoses is to satisfy the world's need for "more love, compassion, and tolerance."[71] He also argued in 2010, "I wouldn't be at all surprised if, within the next five to ten years, the statistics of autism's incidence in children doesn't leap to 1 in 10."[72] However, in the ten years since that prediction the number has come to settle on about 2 percent. On top of that, most of the increase in diagnoses is based on greater understanding and wider diagnostic criteria. As yet it is easier to diagnose autism in children than in adults. The change in criteria between the 1980s and 2010s meant I was only diagnosed as an adult.

Stillman's emphasis on Reiki is contradicted by the U.S. bishops, who state, "Neither the Scriptures nor the Christian tradition as a whole speak of the natural world as based on 'universal life energy' [as Reiki claims] that is subject to manipulation by the natural human power of thought and will."[73]

---

70 Stillman, chap. six: "A Remarkable Revelation."

71 Stillman, *Autism and the God Connection*, chap. one: "Making Miracles."

72 Stillman, *The Autism Prophecies*, Introduction.

73 Committee on Doctrine of the USCCB, "Guidelines for Evaluating Reiki as an Alternative Therapy" (United States Conference of Catholic Bishops, March 25, 2009), para. 9, https://www.usccb.org/resources/evaluation-guidelines-finaltext-2009-03_0.pdf.

A line from the 2003 Vatican document on the New Age grasps the cornucopia of different ideas Stillman mentions throughout his books: "An adequate Christian discernment of New Age thought and practice cannot fail to recognize that . . . it represents something of a compendium of positions that the Church has identified as heterodox."[74] The same Vatican document also points out the underlying problem with Stillman: "The fundamental difficulty of all New Age thought is that this transcendence is strictly a self-transcendence to be achieved within a closed universe."[75] Even when talking about good Catholic practices like the young boy leaving his Batman figurine for Mary, he ultimately has a closed, reductionist, non-Christian worldview. Stillman has a few useful reflections, but ultimately, we must reject his position on autistic spirituality.

We who are autistic know that we are "wonderfully made" as the Psalmist says (see Ps 139:14). We know that God made us in his image and likeness (see Gen 1:26). We know that before God formed us in the womb, he knew us and loved us (see Jer 1:5). I hope the meditations that make up the rest of this book will help you to see your wonderful autistic self as God made you. I invite you to continue reading to see how *God loves the autistic mind*.

---

74 Pontifical Council for Culture and Pontifical Council for Interreligious Dialogue, "Jesus Christ The Bearer Of The Water Of Life: A Christian Reflection on the New Age" (Vatican, February 2, 2003), sec. 1.4, https://www.vatican.va/roman_curia/pontifical_councils/interelg/documents/rc_pc_interelg_doc_20030203_new-age_en.html.

75 Ibid., sec. 6.2.

Part Two

52 Meditations for Autistics
and Those Who Love Us

BEFORE DIVING INTO the first meditation, I want to explain the format, so you feel comfortable. To help us stay grounded, each meditation will have the same outline. The theme we will pray about is composed of four sections. The idea is to dedicate ten to fifteen minutes of quiet time to read and reflect on the material.

The meditation begins with a story. Often this is a story from the life of an autistic Christian. As the author, many of the stories are from my own life. Some are from people I have talked to, and some are historical Christians who might have been autistic. Other stories may not involve autistics but have lessons for us.

Second comes a Bible passage that will be particularly helpful for the topic. I have used the *Revised Standard Version*, second Catholic edition (RSV:2CE) as I like its literal and accurate translation.

Third comes a reflection in which I write a little about the topic from a spiritual perspective. This includes my experience and the experience of those I've talked to.

Finally, each meditation ends with a short prayer. This provides a few lines that are ideal to use at the end of your reflection time.

God Protects Me

1. God Sees the Whole of Me

Story

Greg Willits hosted a radio show that was live fifteen hours a week for four years. He and his wife filled most of the time with occurrences from everyday life, but they would also often have interviews, where he admits his preparation was often brief.

To Greg and his wife, autism had become "not so much an adversity to overcome as much as it was something that was the core of their children, ingrained in their personalities and infused in their very beings."[76] He notes that it would be hard to see his sons without autism.

On one show he had a guest who also had an autistic child. He asked the guest, "If a cure for autism was discovered, wouldn't you *miss* some part of your child's personality that was caused by

---

76 Greg Willits, "Our Own Unique Crosses," in *Special Children, Blessed Fathers: Encouragement for Fathers of Children with Special Needs*, ed. Randy Hain (Steubenville, OH: Emmaus Road Publishing, 2015), 80.

autism?"[77] The guest flipped out. Greg notes that he was glad it was a phone interview, for otherwise it might have come to blows.

Greg remarked later that this incident helped him realize that his autistic children have been a blessing. He also realized that some parents can struggle more with children who have higher support needs.

What do we imagine God's perspective would be? God is a good Father looking benevolently down on all his children, seeing their whole person and marveling at it. If autism is part of who that person is, God sees that too and does so with love, inviting us into his heart as autistics.

Passage

> Keep me as the apple of the eye;
> hide me in the shadow of your wings,
> from the wicked who despoil me,
> my deadly enemies who surround me (Ps 17:8–9).

Reflection

We can think that we need to hide our autism. If I'm going to a big event at the cathedral or an academic conference, I often need to minimize some autistic behaviors to not create a scene. Even though I'm public about my diagnosis, at times I'm still a little embarrassed by my autistic traits. I feel that pulling out a stim toy or rocking back and forth would be looked down on by those around me.

---

77 Ibid., 82.

However, God's viewpoint is totally different. He sees me as the apple of his eye. As Summer Kinard notes, "Disabilities do not embarrass God. Rather they are for our salvation and to reveal the glory of God."[78]

In fact, the Hebrew word translated here as "apple" refers more to the pupil. God keeps us in the center or focus of his eye. He sees each part of us; he sees us in our totality, and he loves us. It is much like when I am looking at pictures of my nephews and niece, I think they are each wonderful and cute. God thinks that each of us is wonderful.

Prayer

Lord, you who look down on me as the apple of your eye, please keep looking upon me with your grace.

2. Jesus Loves Me as an Autistic

Story

In 2014, the Vatican hosted a conference on autism. It was run by the Pontifical Council for Health Care Workers, so most talks focused on that. However, Father Andrzej Kiciński instead focused on how we can apply theology to religious education of autistics. He began with a testimony from Domenico, who is autistic and in his twenties.

---

78 Summer Kinard, *Of Such Is the Kingdom: A Practical Theology of Disability* (Chesterton, IN: Ancient Faith Publishing, 2019), 18.

Domenico notes, "I am seriously thinking about the fact of why an autistic person is called to life. It is really worthwhile thinking about this. I thought that there could be no meaning to this call for autistic people, the mentally defective, and the mad. But I have second thoughts. And this is not my opinion. Now I fight for an autistic life. I believe that it has a meaning. I alert all autistic people not to lose faith in their lives. Autistic people are as important as other people. I cry out: the autistic manage to love, to think, to believe in God, to be ashamed. They are sensitive people. They weep in loneliness."[79]

It is true that autistics are more likely to be atheists, but this does not mean that God forgot about us. Instead, we have a life that God values: like Domenico, we sometimes just need clarity to realize how much God loves us as autistics.

Passage

"The LORD sees not as man sees; man looks on the outward appearance, but the LORD looks on the heart" (1 Sam 16:7).

Reflection

So often we humans focus on what is external. We see someone who is attractive or someone who seems to look most pious

---

79 Andrzej Kiciński, "The Theological Foundations of Religious Education for People with Autism Spectrum Disorder," in *Proceedings of the XXIX International Conference: The Person with Autism Spectrum Disorders: Animating Hope*, vol. XXIX.3, Dolentium Hominum (The Person with Autism Spectrum Disorders: Animating Hope, New Synod Hall, Vatican City: Pontifical Council for Health Care Workers, 2014), 83.

during Mass as the holiest. God instead looks at our heart. We might be putting all our effort into living the Mass in a holy way, but we might still seem fidgety to others because we are stimming constantly to make it through.

God, however, does not focus on those external aspects but peers into our heart. How is our heart directed? Are we putting in our best effort to pray or are we just trying to look the part? We autistics don't always show our dedication to God in the same way as others. We often must struggle more to carry out even the ordinary acts of Catholicism, like participating in Sunday Mass. But God sees that dedication in the heart, and even our stimming during Mass is seen as a positive.

Remember that God sees our heart and how dedicated we are. He doesn't focus on what we might look like externally. As such, we need not worry if our external aspects don't quite match the image of holiness another person might have.

Prayer

Lord, you know my heart, you know how much I love you even if others don't see it. Jesus, lead my heart to your heart, let me see you fully as you are.

3. Jesus Wants My Heart

Story

During my second year of engineering, listening to John Paul II, I felt a call to be a priest. I felt Jesus whispering to me internally, "I want you to be my priest." I thought about being a priest with a few different religious communities: one was the Legionaries of Christ. I went to visit the Legion's house of formation and fell in love. On my first weekend visit, I was set to join in the summer. I didn't feel like I was doing anything amazing. I just knew that God wanted me there.

However, as I began novitiate a few months later, I really started feeling bad. Part of it was difficulty adjusting, part of it was seeing that all those who went to the high school seminary looked way better than me, part of it was seeing my own defects more clearly, and part of it may even have been depression. For example, my handwriting was so bad that I needed to do remedial exercises out of a book made for elementary school students.

I felt horrible, but the novice master kept reminding me of that call, and that God wanted me to be his priest. He didn't tell me I was perfect, but that God wanted me even with my imperfections and sinful nature.

After a few months, the darkness cleared, and I again was able to see how God wanted me to be a Legionary priest. I also realized that part of what I assumed was holiness was simply what some had learned of Legionary life in high school. I have now been a Legionary priest since 2013.

Passage

For I am the least of the apostles, unfit to be called an apostle, because I persecuted the Church of God. But by the grace of God I am what I am, and his grace toward me was not in vain (1 Cor 15:9–10).

Reflection

Sister Marie Paul Curley, FSP, felt an inadequacy in standing up to the model of Saint Paul in her religious life, just as I felt inadequate in my seminary life. Later, she reflected on how she would look at Saint Paul from a distance and put him on a pillar, yet as she read more and more of his works, he seemed far more human.

Sister Curley reflected, "Our feelings of inadequacy can make us forget that being called is not about being worthy. It is about being loved. None of us is worthy of our sacred baptismal vocation to be Christ for others."[80]

We autistics often struggle with inadequacy as we don't measure up to the standards of the neurotypical world. Many neurotypicals look for their fulfillment in relationships and spend their free time socializing about nothing in particular. We are often not like that. In fact, Jesus is happy with me being the best me I can be. Forcing myself to be a social butterfly or the life of the party is not the best me. Instead, the best me for others, for my happiness, and for Jesus might be me sitting in a library studying some arcane theological point to finish my doctorate.

Prayer

Lord, you are the source of joy and happiness, you desire my fulfillment more than I can even desire it myself. Help me to accept myself as you accept me, just as I am, and to find happiness in that.

---

80 Marie Paul Curley, *See Yourself Through God's Eyes: 52 Meditations to Grow in Self-Esteem* (Boston, MA: Pauline Books and Media, 2009), 24.

4. I Believe in You, Jesus

Story

One of my favorite movies is *Good Will Hunting*. Will Hunting is a mathematical genius who can easily solve problems that math professors find almost impossible. He is gifted, and his brain does not seem fully neurotypical.

He starts out as a janitor at MIT in Boston, when the professors discover him answering problems they put up as challenges for students. One professor takes him under his wing. Slowly, his talent becomes more evident. He is set to become a top math professor.

However, at the climax, he gets up and drives across the country. What had happened? The girl who he'd developed a relationship with was continuing her education on the West Coast and that was more important that whatever tutelage this professor could give. That relationship mattered most.

I often think of this final scene as me leaving engineering to enter the seminary because I had found a relationship with God worth leaving all that behind for. I was willing to give up a well-paying job that I would likely enjoy because I have a personal relationship with him who is love itself.

Passage

If you confess with your lips that Jesus is Lord and believe in your heart that God raised him from the dead, you will be saved. For man believes with his heart and so is justified, and he confesses with his lips and so is saved (Rom 10:9–10).

Reflection

We often think of Jesus as some historical figure, but unlike Caesar or Plato, he does not just live in history. He lives in each of us who believe.

Every Sunday we repeat in the Creed: "I believe in one God... I believe in one Lord Jesus Christ... I believe in the Holy Spirit...." In repeating this, we are reminded that the Trinity is alive. We profess this belief personally, not simply as a nameless member of a collective but with a definitive "I believe."

We can often focus on God as a principle, especially as autistics, but God is a person that we personally relate to. We can—and should—develop a personal relationship with the three persons of the Trinity.

Philosophy can determine that there was a first principle, but philosophy alone can't lead us to the three persons of the Trinity. We don't need to believe to have a first cause, but we need to believe in a Trinity.

The *Catechism of the Catholic Church* describes faith (150): "Faith is first of all a personal adherence of man to God. At the same time, and inseparably, it is a free assent to the whole truth that God has revealed. As personal adherence to God and assent to his truth, Christian faith differs from our faith in any human person."

Many times, it is recommended to make an act of faith and renew our commitment when we begin prayer. This is valuable as it reminds us of the relationship that we have with the one we speak with in prayer.

Prayer

Act of Faith

O Trinity, I believe that you are Father, Son, and Holy Spirit. I believe that the Son came to die for our sin and set us free. I personally believe all that you are and all that you teach through the Church.

5. The Good Shepherd

Story

In 2013, researchers interviewed seventy-eight autistics active in the Dutch Reformed Church and found that, on average, they had more negative views of God than did equally active neurotypicals.[81] Temple Grandin noted above that she sees God more as a moral lawgiver or principle than a companion and friend. This means that we often have to put more effort into a positive outlook on God.

Catherine, an autistic woman, gave me a similar testimony, "As a kid, God was presented to me as a vengeful, abusive authority figure who demanded specific things/couldn't abide non-perfections, and would (regretfully? gleefully?) put me back in line by hurting me in some manner. That any error of any type made everything useless or irredeemable; I was flawed so I was useless and disgusting."

---

81 Cf. Hanneke Schaap-Jonker et al., "Autism Spectrum Disorders and the Image of God as a Core Aspect of Religiousness," *The International Journal for the Psychology of Religion* 23, no. 2 (April 1, 2013): 145–60, https://doi.org/10.108 0/10508619.2012.688005.

Later Catherine learned to enjoy the gifts that God was granting her, like chocolate and warm sweaters. She also learned not to judge when her reaction didn't match what others thought was the right reaction. She notes, "Most of my prayer is informal talking to God—literally rambling at Him—tying daily experiences into bigger reality. It might be about my lace-making, then I make a comment on how the lace is 'hole-y,' and I snicker because I made a pun and assume God or at least my guardian angel was too." God is a good Father who laughs with us, not a punishing force who laughs at us.

Passage

The LORD is my shepherd, I shall not want . . .
Even though I walk through
the valley of the shadow of death,
I fear no evil;
for you are with me;
your rod and your staff,
they comfort me (Ps 23:1, 4).

Reflection

When we read Psalm 23, we see how God is a shepherd, but not just any shepherd, the most wonderful shepherd who cares immensely for his sheep.

A sheep needs several things: it needs grass and water to eat and drink, it needs companionship with the other sheep and the shepherd, and it needs protection. The psalm relates how the Lord as the good shepherd provides for each of these needs.

Verse two indicates that the Lord leads us to fulfill the need for grass and food; verse three talks about companionship; and verse four indicates that he'll keep us safe. However, the Lord being the good shepherd does not stop at what we need to survive but looks to what could build us up. He prepares a banquet and gives us so much that our cup overflows. We autistics need to avoid a mere transactional relationship with God.

Ultimately, God is not just okay or kind of good, but he is the source of all goodness. We can easily reduce God to one more good person, but every good person is good inasmuch as he or she is like God, whose goodness is beyond all other good people's goodness combined.

Prayer

Jesus, I know you said, "I am the good shepherd; I know my own and my own know me" (Jn 10:14). Please remember me and help me to know your goodness better.

6. Mary, My Mother

Story

My mom graduated top of her class in engineering, but she gave up that field to raise me and my sisters. As a kid I did not realize how much she had given up just to be there when I came home and went to my room to stim and read about dinosaurs.

Mom was always caring and treated us all with respect. I live across the country, but all my sisters, after moving out and living on the other side of town or two hours away, decided to return and live on the same street as my parents within about half a mile.

When I was about ten months old, a recession hit the city, so my dad's small business was struggling. Mom decided to go back to work. However, when she left the house every morning, I would scream bloody murder. (I'm relying on her story, as I don't remember this age.) This went on for a few months until mom could not take it anymore, since she cared for me so much. She has stayed home ever since.

She was strict in some ways. For example, we never had candy or sweet bakery stuff except on Sundays and birthdays, but her overarching characteristic was her kindness. As I grew up, I was taught about Mary as the perfect mother. Although my mom isn't perfect, I could easily see many of Mary's traits in my own mom.

Passage

When Jesus saw his mother, and the disciple whom he loved standing near, he said to his mother, "Woman, behold, your son!" Then he said to the disciple, "Behold, your mother!" (Jn 19:26–27)

Reflection

Jesus is not only with us: he gives us the best mother to care for us. Mary watches over us and guides us like a good mother. Just as you might ask the holy old woman at your parish to pray for you, we ask the holiest woman in the whole Church to pray for us.

Seeing Mary helps us see the humanity of Jesus. He has a mother like we do. He gives us this mother to be our mother too. She is the most caring mother who is constantly looking out for us. We can see her helping us to focus during prayer, talking to us about a decision we are unsure of, helping us find the right vocation, and so much more.

Some of us had caring parents like mine, and some might struggle more because it is harder to relate God the Father and

Mary to our parents. Reading online stories, I see some autistics who struggled because their parents never accepted their autism. In such a situation, we can proceed by negation. We take away the meanness, the vindictiveness, the pettiness of our parents to get a sense of what God and Mary are like. Even if we had good parents, we could go further along this path: Mary is a caring mother beyond the caring of any other mother. We distinguish God the Father and Mary as parents whose goodness exceeds the goodness of all the best parents combined.

Prayer

Mary, mother of Jesus and my mother, watch over me and guide me, pray for me, a sinner, now and at the hour of my death.

Entering the Lord's Presence

7. God's Peace Overpowers

Story

So often as autistic people we get stressed by things everyone else considers just normal; but then we can also have days where everything goes right to give us great peace. Sometimes we have such a great peace that even something that would normally bother us doesn't.

I don't need the exact same schedule each day, but once a schedule is made, I really don't like to change it. I do an annual week-long silent retreat and one day I felt so much peace, that schedule changes didn't worry me.

I was supposed to have thirty minutes off after a talk to say my daily Mass (about twenty-five minutes) and two and a half hours off in the afternoon to go on a nice long bike ride on a beautiful path nearby, but in about ten minutes both evaporated. The talk went ten minutes over, so I had to reschedule Mass. Then, as I was leaving, I was asked to lead an optional prayer that I had planned on skipping: this made it impossible to do my planned bike ride.

Usually, this would have led to a snarky comment—probably telling the person to forget about me leading that prayer—but on this day Jesus had given me so much peace that I just said, "Okay."

Passage

"Peace I leave with you; my peace I give to you; not as the world gives do I give to you. Let not your hearts be troubled, neither let them be afraid" (Jn 14:27).

Reflection

So often we can know the things that get us going and can trigger a meltdown—hence, we generally avoid them. We rely on our own strength. But sometimes we need to be aware that Jesus can give us strength to get through them.

I wouldn't intentionally seek out triggers for meltdowns, but once they start coming beyond my control, I turn to Jesus. Jesus can give me peace to carry on through them.

As we grow spiritually, we become more continually aware of Jesus' presence in our lives. This doesn't eliminate difficulties, but it does keep us at a level of peace where they don't drive us crazy. Even though we have our same struggles, Jesus can help our baseline anxiety be two or three out of ten rather than the five to seven we autistics can tend toward. Then, even bumping up two or three points doesn't overwhelm us.

Prayer

Jesus, Prince of Peace, bring peace to my restless soul. Help me to recognize you in my life and receive the peace you want to give me. Lead me not into anxiety but to the freedom of the children of

God. Help me to get through all my struggles today without a meltdown—to lay my troubles at your feet instead. Amen.

8. Leaving Our Stress in God's Hands

Story

Once, I was cleaning up before our provincial came to visit for lunch. (A provincial is basically for religious priests what a bishop is for diocesan priests.) I was using a leaf-blower on the sidewalk and accidentally blew a bunch of leaves and some dirt from the sidewalk onto the car of another member of my community. (I did not think through the whole process, and this was an honest mistake.)

He came out part way through my cleaning and moved the car, blocking mine in. When I asked him to move it right after lunch, he said I needed to clean his car off perfectly before he moved it.... But I had to go out right afterward. I was overcome with worry.

I spent the whole lunch meeting with our provincial worrying about how I was going to clean that car fast enough to get to my other appointment. Because I was so worried, I really wasn't focused while our provincial told us about all kinds of wonderful things happening.

It turns out that this was nothing: he was just joking and was satisfied with ten seconds of hosing the side of his car. He thought his joking was obvious, but I missed his nonverbal signs.

Passage

Cast your burden on the LORD, and he will sustain you; he will never permit the righteous to be moved (Ps 55:22).

Reflection

Everyone can be overcome with worries, but we on the spectrum have a particular difficulty because we can get anxious over things that others don't worry about. In the story above, I'm guessing most neurotypicals would have gotten his non-verbal cues and known that he wasn't insisting on a detailed cleaning.

Sarah Ball wrote a book on anxiety and Christian prayer. She notes, "Understanding that fear was created by God for our protection will allow us to accept fear as God's design, versus resisting and running from it. It will also bring us closer to the original purpose of fear, which is worship."[82]

Once we realize that our worries were created to protect us, we can ask what we need protecting against. We developed worries to protect us from deadly animals in the jungle, but now those same worries concern us with things like an event this week in a non-sensory-friendly environment. We aren't sure if someone will say yes to a favor we ask of them, or we are worried we'll be late. These types of worries are helped so much by being given over to the Lord so he can take care of them. (Sometimes even writing these down helps. I know if I'm distracted with worry about something I have to do while praying, I am often calmed by writing it in my to-do app.) Holding on to these types of worries only makes them worse.

Ball also mentioned that fear leads us to worship. The fear of the Lord is almost the opposite of a worrisome fear. Fear of the Lord is a realization of God's greatness over all: it is a mix of awe, marvel, and admiration. This fear is linked to love and worship.

---

82 Sarah E. Ball, *Fearless in 21 Days: A Survivor's Guide to Overcoming Anxiety* (New York, NY: FaithWords, 2018), 18.

When we cast our worries on the Lord, we grow in fear of him because we see his greatness better.

Prayer

Holy Lord God of hosts, who fill heaven and earth with your glory, take my worries upon your shoulders and vanquish them.

9. God's Abundance

Story

The prophet Ezekiel was given a vision of God's overabundant goodness (cf. Ezek 47:1–12). He was taken to the entrance of the Temple and saw water flowing from the eastern side of the Temple out into the Judean desert. Naturally, this area is dry as stone and quite steep with a 5,200-foot drop toward the Dead Sea in under twenty miles. (The road down to Jericho still exists today, and when I drove it, I could see how it was the setting for being robbed at the beginning of the parable of the Good Samaritan.)

At first, Ezekiel saw just a little water coming out of the temple, but the man with him measured off 500 yards, and the stream was ankle deep, then 500 more, then 500 more, then 500 more, and at 2,000 yards from the Temple, no one could pass through it. The water, representing God's grace, was multiplying. Ezekiel saw trees beside the river, which was swarming with fish. Fishermen were fishing and the water brought joy to everyone.

The most amazing point is that this water was so fresh that it would somehow make the water of the Dead Sea fresh. The Dead Sea is much saltier than the ocean: when I went there the salt was almost overwhelming.

This parable of Ezekiel reminds us that God is over-abundant in his blessings. He doesn't just give us the blessings we need, but blessing upon blessing more than we need.

Passage

How precious to me are your thoughts, O God!
How vast is the sum of them!
If I would count them, they are more than the sand.
When I awake, I am still with you (Ps 139:17–18).

Reflection

It is easy to see the rationality of our world needing a creator, a first cause. We call this person God. However, what is beyond what we can reason is a God who comes down to us as a man, a God who gives us an overabundance of graces, a God who shares his inner thoughts. That is something many humans struggle with.

Why does God give us such abundance? Out of love. Think about a man who is in love. When he goes by the flower section in the supermarket, he stops and examines them for ten minutes to figure out which bouquet his beloved would like more. No flowers are needed, and he could probably get by with any bouquet, but he wants the best for his beloved. I remember seeing my dad do this. If mom asked us to pick up something at the grocery store on the way home, we'd always come out with two extra things: chips and salsa (his favorite snack), and a bouquet of flowers for mom. He'd pull out two or three, get input from us kids—especially my sister, who was way better at such things—and then take them home for mom.

Likewise, God is madly in love with each of us and wants to lavish an overflowing abundance of grace on us. God loves us without limits.

Prayer

Lord, you overflow with love and grace, giving beyond what is needed, beyond what we can measure. Allow me to live in that overabundance.

10. Seeing God in Creation

Story

I like to hike or bike through nature. Mountains make an especially potent experience. When I get to the top and look out, I can only marvel at the God who made such a view. Paintings or photos can't capture how the view from atop a mountain completely overwhelms the eyes. You look out and see the mountains rolling in magnificent folds with maybe a small town or lake in the middle.

Once during my community vacation, I decided to do a mountain hiking challenge near the cabin where we were staying. On most of the hikes, I had gone with someone from the community, but on this day I was hiking up a mountain alone and saw only a handful of people the whole way up. When I got to the top, I looked out on a 360 degree view of the surrounding mountains and lakes. I thought about what a wonderful God we have who created this; he not only created this in general, God created this for me.

Another time, as I was driving through a park, I was overwhelmed with the beauty God put in nature when an adolescent black bear walked across the road ten yards in front of me. God could have created the world just to fulfill practical needs, but instead he made it beautiful and gave us minds to see that beauty.

Passage

"Bless the Lord, all works of the LORD,
sing praise to him and highly exalt him for ever. . . .
Let the earth bless the LORD;
let it sing praise to him and highly exalt him for ever"
(Dan 3:35, 52).[83]

Reflection

The whole of creation blesses the Lord. Seeing the intricate detail of a leaf or the wondrous strength of an oak can lead us to see God as the master of detail or the source of strength far beyond what the leaf or the tree display. Throughout the Bible analogies like this are used: "The LORD is my rock" (Ps 18:2); "The kingdom of heaven is like a grain of mustard seed" (Mt 13:31); "He is like a tree planted by the streams of water, that yields its fruit in its season" (Ps 1:3); "Are not five sparrows sold for two pennies? And not one of them is forgotten before God" (Lk 12:6).

All non-rational creatures—from the lowliest piece of gravel to highest flying eagle—glorify God by existing and following their nature. They are taken care of intimately by God.

From the use of natural reason, including autistic pattern recognition, we can work from the multitude of created things to the unique first cause in God. We can see that everything else is contingent, but God is the only necessary being. Without that one necessary being, none of us contingent beings would exist. The Church teaches that we can know God from what we see in nature

---

83 Some Bibles will list this as Dan 3:57, 74.

and natural reason. This reason alone does not show us the incarnation or the interior life of the Trinity, but it does show us God as a loving creator who leaves us an unfathomably beautiful natural world. As noted above, the *Handbook of Christian Apologetics* by Kreeft and Tacelli gave solid rational explanations and was one of the books that helped me most.

Prayer

God, creator of the heavens, of the earth, of the seas and all creatures dwelling on the earth, show yourself to me through the beauty of this world.

11. Facts Help Us Enter God's Presence

Story

In the seminary, I got the nickname Schneider-pedia. It was made in jest, and it wasn't 100 percent positive, as I could unload so many facts and details in conversation that others were overwhelmed. After I had been diagnosed with autism, I realized that this is normal for autistics and it even has a name: infodumping.

But it felt different when I brought facts to prayer. These facts were not an obstacle to conversing with God. He never seemed to interrupt and say he had enough. He never seemed surprised by facts or wondered why I remembered some random connection from a documentary I watched four years ago.

God seemed to want whatever way I communicated even if it was infodumping. He didn't criticize this overabundance of facts. He even seemed to respond in kind, coming back to remind me of more facts.

Passage

If Christ has not been raised, then our preaching is in vain and your faith is in vain (1 Cor 15:14).

Reflection

Most religions throughout history were made by man and based on half-truths. Take the Greek gods for example: there is a truth that there are powers beyond what a Greek of 500 BC could fully understand or control: the sun rose and set daily, waves splashed about, and lightning came down. So far it is 100 percent true. But, when they attribute these actions to Apollo, Poseidon, and Zeus respectively, they mix in error. These are not personified gods, but natural realities controlled by an all-powerful God.

Many religions also talk about their deities living in a mythical pre-history or an alternate dimension. A few others claim their gods walked around in historical time. But we Christians know that God became man in time. He died, he rose, and he sits at the right hand of the Father, where he will judge us at the end of time. Christianity is based on such historical facts as the resurrection and the continuity of the Church since the twelve apostles.

We can take into prayer all the facts in our autistic memory. We can take the facts about the saints, about the Bible, about the history of the Church. Each of these facts can help connect us with God. Our tendency to overshare facts when conversing can actually be an advantage in prayer, since each of those facts can be a point of contact leading us closer to God. We can build something of a web of connections with God.

We often think of prayer as simply a single line back and forth. There is a main line of communication, but we can support this with a bunch of little connections made by each connecting fact.

Prayer

Father, Lord of light and truth, let your truth shine upon me and enlighten me in all I do, so I can do it following the truth that you yourself are.

12. From Loneliness to Being Alone with God

Story

Katie, an autistic woman, told me about her prayer. She noted, "For me prayer is part of the constant monologue/dialogue I have going on in my head. If I am not directing my thoughts/words to myself then I am directing them to Jesus. I have always talked to Jesus as a friend or brother."

Katie also struggles with vocal prayer and can't lead a prayer in a group. She feels like she'd be directing a monologue to someone right in front of her that should really be a dialogue. It feels fake and artificial as when a head of state, who's no great friend of the pope, reads a formal greeting that makes it sound like he's the pope's best friend.

She wonders about some prayers. People seem to describe what they are doing rather than do it. She notes that when we say, "We pray for . . .", we are stating that we are praying, which makes it seem less a prayer. It's as if we greeted someone, "I am greeting John Smith." She asks, "How is saying it is right and just to give thanks actually the same as really and truly thanking God?" For Katie, prayer is personal conversation, not something in which you need to explain what you are doing. It is not like an instructional video on YouTube.

Passage

"I will not leave you desolate; I will come to you. . . . Let not your hearts be troubled, neither let them be afraid" (Jn 14:18, 27).

Reflection

Autism often leads to misunderstanding and loneliness. We want more friends to play *Catan* or *Dungeons and Dragons* with us, but often difficulties in communication mean that we are alone more than we want to be. We can also struggle in similar ways with romance. We start feeling lonely.

In our loneliness, we can turn to the one who is always ready to talk to us, God, the Father, Son, and Spirit. Jesus promised at the Last Supper not to leave us alone; he tells us not to be afraid. We can know he will always be available.

In pagan religions, gods are capricious. Jupiter or Loki might listen to you or not, but they definitely aren't your friend. But in Christianity, God has promised us that he will be with us always. Our hearts need not fear rejection, loneliness, or sorrow, for he is at our side. He is there both to protect us with his strength but also to care for us as a family member or friend. God is always beside us if we want to talk. He's always there to lend a shoulder when we need one from a friend.

Prayer

Jesus, friend of all humankind, friend of sinners, friend of mine, help me in my loneliness, stay with me, fill my heart with your love.

Autistic Is as Jesus Planned

13. In God's Eyes, Being Autistic Is Not Wrong

Story

My drive home from the psychologist after receiving an autism diagnosis was tough. I'd recently had a major fail for the first time in my life. Now, this. It seemed like a sentence to constantly be a failure as a priest. In my head, I probably said a few words priests shouldn't say.

Once I got home, I immediately went on Amazon and picked up a bunch of books. I devoured them. I currently have a whole shelf of autism books, yet I think I have more of them on Kindle. As I read, I started to see my whole past life, I started to understand things that were confusing in the past. Suddenly, a lot of my life made sense.

It took me a few months to come to terms with being autistic, but I think I did. I realize now that this is a gift God gave me. Sure, at times it is a cross, but every person has crosses: I now know clearly what my own cross is.

Passage

> For you formed my inward parts,
> you knitted me together in my mother's womb.
> I praise you, for I am wondrously made.
> Wonderful are your works!
> You know me right well (Ps 139:13–14).

Reflection

God made us wonderfully. He made us wonderfully autistic. From before time, God had each of us in his mind with all our natural strengths and defects. The *Catechism of the Catholic Church* (364) teaches that God makes our whole being in his image and likeness. We can often reduce this just to the soul or just to what might be considered "normal." However, even our autistic aspects are made in God's image and likeness. God looks on our autistic brain with love.

Christianity is unique in recognizing how wonderful people are and what dignity they have no matter what their mental or physical condition. The Church fights for the human dignity of every person from the newly conceived baby to the patient with Alzheimer's who can't even remember his or her spouse's face anymore, from the Olympic athlete to the autistic who needs full time support. Father Andrzej Kiciński mentioned this in the Vatican conference on autism: "This originality of Christianity is expressed in the fact that whereas people with autism are seen as weak and sick by other people, before God, instead, they are great because of what they are."[84]

---

84 Kiciński, "The Theological Foundations of Religious Education for People with Autism Spectrum Disorder," 85.

We might think that autism is only negative or only suffering, but we can often enjoy certain things more, and find happiness in things that others might not. Temple Grandin noted, "Happy [autistic] people are the ones who have satisfying work in their lives that's connected to an area of strong interest. I realize it's difficult for a lot of parents to understand that their child with ASD may derive greater happiness through work or hobbies than through pure emotional bonding, or that marriage or family may not be the top of his list of priorities. It's still happiness, nonetheless."[85] God wants our happiness as autistic people, even if that happiness is not the same as others' happiness.

Prayer

Lord, who made me in your image and likeness, who formed me in my mother's womb to be autistic, help me to accept this and find happiness in this.

14. Thanking God for Autism

Story

After I made my autism diagnosis public, I got a message from a lady who had seen my video on a Facebook group for moms raising autistic kids. She had been in my class all through elementary school and now helps coordinate the sensory-friendly Mass back in my hometown.

---

85 Temple Grandin and Sean Barron, *The Unwritten Rules of Social Relationships: Decoding Social Mysteries Through the Unique Perspectives of Autism*, 1st edition (Arlington, TX: Future Horizons, 2005), 46.

I had to ask her to reflect on what she remembered from elementary school. Looking back, did I seem autistic now that she knows the reality of her son? Her response was that nobody talked about autism back in the '80s or early '90s. When I look back, I see a few times where if the DSM-5 criteria existed back then, I would have been diagnosed.

At the same time, when I was diagnosed, the psychologist told me two things beyond my diagnosis. First, that under the DSM-IV, I would be diagnosed with Asperger's, and second, that had I stayed in computer engineering I probably never would have been diagnosed.

Despite the small amount of stigma that I've faced, I think being diagnosed has ultimately been a blessing. Now I understand so much of my past. Now I understand why certain things are difficult. Now I can situate myself within priestly ministry more in accord with my talents and defects.

Passage

Jesus declared, "I thank you, Father, Lord of heaven and earth, that you have hidden these things from the wise and understanding and revealed them to infants" (Mt 11:25).

Reflection

The word translated "infants" in this verse is not one of the standard Greek words for child or infant. Instead, νήπιος (pronounced: nēpios) etymologically derives from "word" or "something spoken" (ἔπος—pronounced epos) together with a negative prefix (equivalent to un- or non- in English). It refers to someone unable to articulate his or her thoughts in speech, or someone who is uneducated.

No matter whether we are verbal or non-verbal, high-IQ or low-IQ, I think it's a universal experience that we autistics have trouble articulating our thoughts. I'm writing a doctoral thesis and I am highly verbal, but even I often struggle to explain my thoughts, to transform what I mean in my mind to sounds from my mouth.

Yet, in this state, Jesus tells us we have been blessed with understanding and revelation of the kingdom of heaven. Jesus is thankful to the Father for this. We too should be thankful for this revelation.

We should also be thankful for being autistic. Beyond that revelation, we have a neurology that gives us many blessings. We are often particularly sensitive to certain sounds or particularly good at doing research, seeing details, or reasoning logically. Autism is a different way of seeing the world, and we should thank God for this vision of the world, even if it isn't the vision that others have.

Prayer

Jesus, thank you for the gift of autism. Thank you for this knowledge, for this way of seeing the world, and even for the aspects that are sometimes a cross for me.

15. My Autistic Identity in Jesus

Story

Summer Kinard is an autistic woman and mother of autistic children. When I asked her about her prayer, she noted, "Personally, I love to chant psalms, read, and meditate on Scriptures late at night, and pray to God and the saints directly in front of icons. To me, God is right here with us. There is no distance. As I joked with a friend, if my prayer rises like incense, God is close enough that he sneezes!"

Summer feels like the Lord is always teaching her, opening her tongue and her ear to his message. She continues, "I feel held and loved by God alongside me. This helps me face hardships because God is next to me where I can know him now, and mystically before me, and healing me in his wake behind me. There is nowhere to go from God's presence. I speak to God simply, directly, though I cannot put into words the love of God, nor do I worry that I should be able to. God knows, because he gives that love and is that love and is the reward and fulfillment of that love. But sometimes I find solace in the call of mourning doves to one another, as though it's the song my heart makes seeking God's face, and I will surely be answered."

All of us Christians find our identity in Jesus, in closeness to him. When we look at the closeness of autistics like Summer, we see that this is the identity of an autistic Christian, a person who communicates with God autistically.

Passage

For I know the plans I have for you, says the LORD, plans for welfare and not for evil, to give you a future and a hope. Then you will call upon me and come and pray to me, and I will hear you (Jer 29:11–12).

Reflection

God always has a personal plan for each person. When that person is autistic, it is an autistic plan. In this way, God confirms our autism and speaks to us in ways appropriate to our specific manifestations of autism.

God hears the prayer of each person, whatever way they communicate that prayer. Autistic ways of communication don't inhibit prayer. This further confirms our autistic identity. The way we communicate with God in autistic English rather than neurotypical or standard English is a big part of our autistic identity in Jesus.

In Jim Sinclair's famous 1993 essay, he explains autistic English. He states, "It takes more work to communicate with someone whose native language isn't the same as yours. And autism goes deeper than language and culture; autistic people are 'foreigners' in any society. . . . You're going to have to learn to back up to levels more basic than you've probably thought about before, to translate, and to check to make sure your translations are understood."[86]

Our language is a large part of our identity. If we communicate with God autistically, that gives us an identity as autistics in our prayer, and also an identity as Christians.

Prayer

Lord Jesus, you know everything, you know that I love you. I communicate that love through my autistic language, and you communicate back adapted to my autism.

---

86 Jim Sinclair, "Don't Mourn For Us," Personal, Jim Sinclair's Website (via Wayback Machine), Originally *Our Voice*, Volume 1, Number 3, 1993, 1993, https://web.archive.org/web/20030118011731/http://web.syr.edu/~jisincla/dontmourn.htm.

16. God Has Wonderful Designs for Me

Story

I easily get frustrated, down and out. I remember one time I was just frustrated because I was not progressing as I would like; I was not able to concentrate due to executive functioning difficulties. My mind was just blank. I went for a jog in the park. The exercise and an audiobook helped clear my head a bit.

Then I saw a fox dart across my path and back into the woods. This wild animal without human care had beautiful bright orange fur despite living in the forest. He jumped in an elegant fluid motion, and then after he was a few feet away, he turned to look at me and jumped away effortlessly.

I thought of how God had given that fox all he needed and did so with elegance. Yet all that fox does is chase squirrels and eat them. God surely provides far more for me. He provided me with much more of a role than controlling the squirrel population and he provides for my needs, too.

Passage

"Why are you anxious about clothing? Consider the lilies of the field, how they grow; they neither toil nor spin; yet I tell you, even Solomon in all his glory was not clothed like one of these. But if God so clothes the grass of the field, which today is alive and tomorrow is thrown into the oven, will he not much more clothe you, O you of little faith?" (Mt 6:28–30).

Reflection

Grant Macaskill reflects on this passage in his book on autism:

> What should, therefore, strike us when Jesus invokes God's providential care for birds and plants is that he does not focus on God's care for productive harvests, and does not use the example of doves or lambs, which could be used in religious worship. His examples involve things with no utility or value (grass and lilies) and things which would be considered unclean (ravens), and he indicates that God cares for and clothes these things in ways that exceed any human ascription of worth.[87]

Our tendency to fail at things that other people find easy can make us autistics seem worthless. But God does not see us as worthless. God does not see us as failures. God provides more than we need, more than we can hope for.

Not only does God provide but he has a wonderful plan for us. Although he clothes the flowers of the field with physical beauty, he clothes us with another kind of beauty. He sets a wonderful path for us to follow in growing toward the fullness of grace. It is a plan that is different for each, but it is a plan than involves our whole selves, including all our autistic traits.

Prayer

Lord, who care for the foxes and the flowers, the trees, and woodpeckers, I know you care for me. Let me see how you care for me.

---

87 Grant Macaskill, *Autism and the Church: Bible, Theology, and Community* (Waco: Baylor University Press, 2019), 78.

17. Imperfections Are Not Sins

Story

Lamar Hardwick, a Baptist pastor, spoke of how his life was changed when he received an autism diagnosis when he was already a pastor: "When I was diagnosed with autism spectrum disorder at age thirty-six, I understood—perhaps for the first time—that I was human. I understood that my years of struggling with certain issues weren't due to a lack of perfection but an abundance of humanity. I learned that I did have some boundaries and some limitations and that I was indeed human. The journey from weakness to strength is one that requires the traveler to accept limitations as well as appreciate progress."[88]

He says that for years he had pushed himself toward an unrealistic ideal. He kept striving for some level of perfection that was beyond him. He would assume that every struggle with social situations, senses, planning, or academics was due to a personal failing. His autism diagnosis allowed him to realize his own weakness. He felt like an overachieving attitude was eating away at his humanity. Without allowing for imperfections, he had been struggling with empathy both for himself and for others.

Now, he feels much more comfortable admitting that he is tired or admitting that he missed something due to his human and autistic limitations.

---

[88] Lamar Hardwick, *I Am Strong: The Life and Journey of an Autistic Pastor*, Kindle (Little Elm, TX: eLectio Publishing, LLC, 2017), 136.

Passage

[I pray to the Father] that according to the riches of his glory he may grant you to be strengthened with might through his Spirit in the inner man, and that Christ may dwell in your hearts through faith; that you, being rooted and grounded in love, may have power . . . to know the love of Christ which surpasses knowledge (Eph 3:16–19).

Reflection

We can often fall into the kind of perfectionism that Dr. Hardwick mentions where we blame every failure on ourselves. Often, though, failures are caused by natural human limitations, not by poor choices or sins. If I miss someone's non-verbal social sign and perform an action based on my misunderstanding, I might consider it an error in hindsight, but it is not a sin.

Reflecting on this passage, Sister Marie Paul Curley notes, "Loving self doesn't mean that we are blind to our faults, but that we accept ourselves as we have been created by God, and we take care of ourselves with gentleness and compassion."[89] God wants us to be filled with his richness, with his glory grounded in love.

One important thing to remember is that we are responsible only for what we choose. If something is beyond our choice, we are not responsible. Sin requires that choice. When things fail beyond our control, this is often a way that God shows us his cross, as he told every Christian to come after him carrying his or her cross.

---

89 Curley, *See Yourself Through God's Eyes*, 44.

Sin is never part of God's plan, but God makes each person with certain human limitations and imperfections.

God is happy that we try our best in prayer, in a social situation, or elsewhere. He knows how he made us and how we might struggle; he doesn't require an absolute vigilance to the point that we become exhausted or paralyzed. Even if it seems like a failure externally, God looks at our heart; he dwells in any heart that loves him.

Prayer

Lord, I know that you love me, help me to love you in return. When I am a failure, look at my heart to see me striving to be like you.

18. Our Stims Are Gifts

Story

I'm into vestibular stimming: rocking back and forth—whether in a chair or between my feet—calms me a lot. Even more if I close my eyes. Since I'm pretty busy with various responsibilities during the day, closing my eyes and rocking isn't often an option.

However, as a priest I do one hour of prayer every morning, which is often a silent, almost-wordless dialogue with God after starting with a Bible passage to reflect on. Thus, I am often able to close my eyes and rock back and forth in a rocking chair or pace for this part.

I'm blessed to able to do this stim. I'm also blessed to have a number of stim toys like tangles and squishy items on my desk. These are not a direct gift from God, but it is a blessing to be able to understand that stimming is healthy and to have the right objects to do so with.

Passage

My God will supply every need of yours according to his riches in glory in Christ Jesus (Phil 4:19).

Reflection

So often, we can look at things that differentiate us from neurotypicals as pure negatives. They can't stand our "fidgeting" that distracts them. We can let their negative judgment overtake us and get nervous about how people might be judging us every time we stim. It's hard to say, but if you've been told to stop a few times, you can get a sense that people don't like it.

I try to do stims that bother others the least. I used to click my pen but found that people would tell me to stop. When I bring a tangle or stress-ball into a meeting and play with it a bit, nobody seems to complain. This is true even when the other meeting participants don't know I'm autistic. (With this being published, I doubt I'll be in many meetings after this where the others don't know I'm autistic.)

We tend to get anxious and nervous about things where others don't, but we also need different things to calm ourselves. In this regard, God is supplying us out of his richness. We need to remember that God provides for each of us: and providing for autistics includes providing stims to calm us.

Prayer

Lord, teach me to appreciate the gifts you give, especially the gifts that show your specific care for me with all my traits. Thank you for creating me this way and thank you again for giving me the means, such as my stim toys, to live this life to the full. Help me to accept who you made me to be and to be the best version of that person, not the best version of someone else.

Personal, Autistic Prayer

19. Understanding God's Mind

Story

I remember in about second grade, in religion class, the teacher taught us that if we asked God for anything in prayer, he would grant it to us. I got excited. I thought about what I wanted, then that night I asked God for a red Ferrari.

I never got the Ferrari. Later, I learned that God often gives us things that are better for us than what we ask for. (Just imagine how dangerous a seven-year-old driving a Ferrari would be: I suspect that had that happened I would have died in a car crash). God is not a giant vending machine in the sky and treating him like that is not a good way to communicate with him.

Instead, I slowly learned to treat God like another person. Obviously, he is a person far more powerful than I am, but he comes down and wants to talk to me one-on-one. So, I speak to him one-on-one, heart-to-heart.

Passage

> Arise, my love, my fair one, and come away.
> O my dove, in the clefts of the rock, in the covert of the cliff,
> let me see your face, let me hear your voice,
> for your voice is sweet, and your face is comely
> (Song 2:13–14).

Reflection

In Christianity, we have a God who is personal. God is not "the Force" or the "unmoved mover." He is a person, who wants a relationship with us. However, as autistics, we often struggle to understand what others are thinking or feeling, and this is often even more difficult with God, as we can't see his face and we don't hear his voice the same way. Our struggles with theory of mind can create a big challenge.

But this challenge can be resolved to bypass theory of mind when we go a little deeper. Once we realize that God speaks in feelings and thoughts directly, we can ask to move to this deeper level. We can in a way bypass theory of mind and speak with Jesus, from his heart to our autistic heart. As such, we know he'll communicate in a way we understand. We need not get overly worried about our struggles in communication with other humans. God communicates directly to the heart.

However, this communication isn't always going to be instantaneously obvious every moment we pray, and sometimes God will seem silent to us. We will have trouble understanding what he wants to communicate to us. That should just encourage us to persevere, knowing by faith that ultimately God will communicate at a deeper level. Prayer is our time with God and sometimes he wants to be with us silently.

Prayer

Jesus, speak to my heart. You know my heart and know the struggles I have with communication, but speaking heart-to-heart can overcome all those difficulties.

20. Prayer Without Words

Story

A young Eastern Orthodox woman named Alexandra told me about her prayer, noting that actions like lighting candles, bowing to an icon, decorating her icon corner with flowers, using prayer beads, and cleaning the church are a big part of her prayer. She felt a special connection to Jesus when she would go into the church on Saturday afternoons to clean the church and prepare vestments for the Sunday morning Divine Liturgy (Mass). She felt a special connection being surrounded by icons of Jesus and the saints. She feels that through this she prays in her actions.

For her, prayer goes beyond the normal acts that we often associate with prayer. She notes, "In praying for others, it frequently works much better if I 'symbolize' other people as little white stones, that I move from one bowl to the next, one by one, as I remember people in prayer."

She also noted how repeating the Jesus prayer during certain actions like planting her vegetable garden can be a big help to turn those otherwise mundane actions into a prayer. Together with her actions-made-prayer, this makes the spiritual immediately accessible to her throughout the day.

Passage

Let love be genuine; hate what is evil, hold fast to what is good; love one another with brotherly affection; outdo one another in showing honor. Never flag in zeal, be aglow with the Spirit, serve the Lord. Rejoice in your hope, be patient in tribulation, be constant in prayer (Rom 12:9–12).

Reflection

Saint Paul is listing off all things all Christians should do. Nowhere in that list is a requirement to speak certain words. In fact, the only mention of speaking in that whole chapter is a mention that people should use their unique gifts for the community, and some of these are about speaking (exhortation, prophecy, and teaching).

In the modern world, we often focus much more on Christian words, whether this is when someone says the sinner's prayer[90] at a Billy Graham rally or when we say "Amen" just before receiving Communion. This focus is on those who can speak, but Jesus wants everyone to be Christian, even those who struggle with speech. I know that as a well-educated autistic man, I struggle more to express myself in words than others do. I am told I use filler words—often "like"—much more than average, and this is me searching for a way to express in words what is in my mind. Summer Kinard mentions this: "It may seem to be a paradox to say

---

90 The 'sinner's prayer' is a common evangelical prayer said at the moment of accepting Jesus into your heart, such as at an altar call. There are several common variations.

that we can love and follow the Word of God without words. Yet, for many people, prayer must often or always be without speech."[91]

God wants us to communicate with him in the way that we can, whether with words or without words. He wants our heart above all else.

Prayer

Jesus, let my actions be my prayer when I don't know words for expressing myself to you. Let my silence speak to you.

21. Keeping God in Our Autistic Memory

Story

In her prayer, Kasandra, an autistic woman, relates best to Jeremiah of all the biblical writers, explaining, "The Word is like fire inside my bones and when I cannot speak or I try to stifle it, it presses like the silent scream of a night terror, weighing on my chest and churning in my thoughts until I can express it in some safe setting."

She feels that prayer is a continuous conversation in which she is constantly remembering Jesus and speaking to him, so much so that she feels she is never alone in her thoughts, but sharing every memory, every thought with God.

She notes, "I've heard others describe prayer as an intentional behavior they have to remember to make time for. I can't relate to

---

91 Kinard, *Of Such Is the Kingdom*, 157.

that. I've heard people say they question the existence of God. I wish I could empathize for their sakes, but in my darkest valleys I couldn't question God's presence or ultimate goodness. I can't imagine living a life in the external world and having to remind myself that an internal/spiritual world exists."

When Jesus asks us to pray always, he is asking us to share our every thought with him, even if those are awkward autistic thoughts that can't really be put into words.

Passage

For I received from the Lord what I also delivered to you, that the Lord Jesus on the night when he was betrayed took bread, and when he had given thanks, he broke it, and said, "This is my body which is for you. Do this in remembrance of me" (1 Cor 11:23–24).

Reflection

We often think of memory as a purely practical aspect of life. A memory is like something in a history book, in an old family photo album or a Facebook "memory." However, for the ancient Jews, memory meant something completely different. They used the term *zikkaron* to indicate a type of memory or memorial that allowed an event to be relived, not merely thought about.

This profound memory is valuable for the Mass, as the one perfect sacrifice of Christ is *re-presented* in unbloody form on the altar.

In our prayer, we can also have a *zikkaron* memory although without the same sacramental realism. We don't just think about an event in Jesus' life, but we relive it with the apostles. Since we autistics often remember a lot of details, we can use them in prayer.

We might return to the Last Supper in our prayer and remember what we read about how they reclined around a low table rather than sitting at a high table like we do. We might remember that for Jesus and the Twelve, there were probably three tables at ninety-degree angles to each other that leave an opening for servers. We might also remember what we read about Palestinian fabrics of the time or probable seating arrangements. We make the memory we have in prayer more real through all these details.

Prayer

Jesus, I remember you. I remember not only a general vision of you, but I see each hair on your head, each wound you got in the passion, each moment of your resurrection appearances.

22. The Validity of My Personal Autistic Prayer

Story

Lucy, an autistic woman, told me of how her prayer didn't match the preconceptions she got from others. She explained, "I had to let go of a lot of preconceived notions of what I thought my relationship with God should be. It's a personal relationship, unique to me (and unique for everyone, of course, but all of my relational experience tends to be different than the experience of those around me)."

She explains the differences in personal prayer based on Jesus' work: "When Christ died, the curtain in the temple was torn in two. The curtain that separated people from God. Before, there were strict laws and procedures that needed to be observed before anyone could approach the Holy God. And even then, it was through the priesthood. Now, I have open access to God through the sacrifice of Jesus and the presence of the Holy Spirit in me. No need for purification because Jesus provides that. When I understood this, I stopped approaching God in a formulaic manner."

One thing that she appreciates about God is that he speaks to her one-on-one the way her husband does; there is no need of the masking she often needs with other human beings. God is available to speak to her in her own way.

Passage

Now there are varieties of gifts, but the same Spirit; and there are varieties of service, but the same Lord; and there are varieties of working, but it is the same God who inspires them all in every one (1 Cor 12:4–6).

Reflection

God gives each person a personality. He gives each person certain gifts, certain talents, and certain difficulties. These present a personal way to pray, a personal path of holiness.

A 2015 study looked at Functional Magnetic Resonance Imaging scans of neurotypical and autistic individuals. The neurotypical brains all had similar conductivity between brain sections when at rest. On the other hand, the autistic brains varied not only from the neurotypical brains, but from each other. Even though we are a small portion of the population, they found much greater variation between different autistic brains than in the neurotypical population.[92] Brain structure is an important factor in determining how we communicate. As prayer is a form of two-way communication, we autistics will vary more in our personal prayer from neurotypicals and from each other.

God is happy with our personal way of praying even if others think it strange. It is like a marriage where the couple seem to be an odd match, but they live a happy marriage. Judging prayer or marriage from outside never gets to what is most important in those intimate relationships. I know that early in my formation as a religious, I struggled with thinking that I did not pray in the "right" way. I did not pray in the way that "holy" brother prayed. Later I learned to be satisfied with my relationship and compare it much less to that of others. (I wish I could say I never compare it, but I need to be honest.)

Prayer

Lord, you come to me in your own way. Let me speak to you in my way. Help me to accept our way of communicating, even if it is not the standard way.

---

92 See Hahamy, A., Behrmann, M. & Malach, R., "The idiosyncratic brain: distortion of spontaneous connectivity patterns in autism spectrum disorder." *Nat Neurosci* 18, 302–309 (2015). https://doi.org/10.1038/nn.3919

23. A Different Viewpoint Can See God

Story

When I had an experience of God as a teenager, I was moved to re-explore my faith. I started looking around at my parish and almost nobody my age seemed sincerely engaged in Church. I had some Protestant friends at that time, and they really seemed more emotionally engaged.

I started thinking that maybe they were right, but I thought I'd check a bit on the Internet. This was early 1998, so social media did not exist, and even the fact that we had internet was more of an exception than the rule. I found a Catholic community through some message boards, most notably OneRock Online Forums.[93] I felt it easier to communicate in these message boards. Suddenly, I was surrounded by a bunch of other Catholics with whom I could share faith experiences. Communication seemed to flow more easily than it did in real life.

After I was diagnosed, I noticed that we autistics tend to find online communication easier. While I was reading a thesis on neurodiversity, I came across the following: "The internet has been used effectively as a prosthetic device by individuals with ASD. Free from distracting environments that make communication

---

93 The original seems lost to time but an archived version from 2002 is available on the Wayback Machine. https://web.archive.org/web/20021213092003/http://board.onerock.com/ (The Wayback Machine also indicates it went offline between 2005 and 2014, with the associated Zine turning into a blog disappearing after 2008). My username – in case any readers remember this message board—was *OLoS* for "Our Lady of Siluva," a lesser-known apparition in Lithuania that converted a town from Protestantism to Catholicism.

more difficult and freer from demands for eye contact and reading social cues, autistics took to the internet to have their voices heard, a phenomenon compared with the development of American Sign Language among the deaf."[94]

Passage

A great and strong wind tore the mountains, and broke in pieces the rocks before the LORD, but the LORD was not in the wind; and after the wind an earthquake, but the LORD was not in the earthquake; and after the earthquake a fire, but the LORD was not in the fire; and after the fire a still small voice. And when Elijah heard it, he wrapped his face in his mantle and went out and stood at the entrance of the cave. And behold, there came a voice to him, and said, "What are you doing here, Elijah?" (1 Kings 19:11–13)

Reflection

God will come in ways we don't expect. I'm sure most of us in Elijah's situation would assume that God was in the earth-shattering wind, the earthquake, or the fire. But God was in the whisper. God does not always follow human logic but reveals himself in unique and unexpected ways.

God's revelation is also affected by the receiver. Each person sees God from a different perspective. When we look at saints like Blessed Solanus Casey or Saint André Bessette, we see people who were probably those least expected to be saints. They were the

---

94 Katie Terry, "Neurodiversity and Autism Spectrum Disorders: Grounding for Social Work Education and Praxis" (Doctor of Social Work, St. Paul, MN, St. Catherine University, 2019), 6, https://sophia.stkate.edu/cgi/viewcontent.cgi?article=1058&context=dsw.

not-so-smart brothers who weren't good at studies or preaching, so they were assigned as the porters or doormen of their respective communities. And in those positions, each managed to bring many people to a deeper faith.

I think that, like these two, we autistics often have a different perspective that helps us see God in a different, but profound way.

Prayer

Jesus, let me see your face with my own eyes. Show yourself to me.

24. Repetition in Prayer

Story

Catherine is an autistic woman who struggles during long periods of prayer, such as dedicating fifteen to thirty minutes to private prayer. However, she notes, "I'll say a decade of the rosary washing dishes, or in a car ride, or what have you. Almost a background stim but using what happen to be prayers."

She finds that these repeated prayers at little moments throughout the day are a great way to connect with God. Catherine notes that often she will pray spontaneously when reading through something, and she'll blurt out, "Hey God, this is pretty neat. What am I doing with this? Or is it just neat? I see you, hiding behind that interesting creature; why else would you make something like that?" After reading more, she might say, "I see you, showing me something about my body that tells me what's going on with something. It's neat. You're neat. I'm going to go get a drink."

Catherine struggles to connect with what she sees as the "normal" way of praying, where you kneel and focus on the person you speak to both in words and in body language. Instead, when she is saying repeated prayers, she is not making eye contact with God or analyzing every word, but the words help her reach a deeper level of communication with God. Sometimes the formal words even give way to a more informal conversation with God.

Passage

He was praying in a certain place, and when he ceased, one of his disciples said to him, "Lord, teach us to pray, as John taught his disciples." And he said to them, "When you pray, say: 'Father, hallowed be your name. Your kingdom come . . .'" (Lk 11:1–2).

Reflection

We can think of the Our Father as just any prayer, but this is precisely how Jesus taught us to pray. (Luke lacks the "Our" in "Our Father," which we are used to from Matthew.) Jesus taught us a simple prayer that can be repeated thousands of times.

Repeating this prayer helps us in various ways. First, it includes all the essential elements of prayer—praise, petition, intercession, and thanksgiving—so we don't overly focus on one of those. Second, since we know the words, we aren't stuck thinking about what to say next: thus, we can more easily go deeper. Third, it can provide us autistics with a certain degree of security—we know exactly what is coming next. I know when I went to a charismatic prayer service, I felt nervous not knowing what was coming, but the Our Father is the exact opposite of that. We know exactly what the next line is. Fourth, referring to God as Our Father reminds us how close he is.

Now the Our Father is not the only prayer we repeat. Many of us say the Hail Mary, the Jesus Prayer, the Glory Be, or some other prayer multiple times a day. The prayers that are commonly repeated in the traditions of the Church are all prayers that have been reflected on long and hard and form a model for Christian prayer. They are also helpful since we know what is coming next. They can almost become a verbal stim since we know them so well.

Prayer

Our Father, who art in heaven . . .

Deep Autistic Prayer

25. Our Senses and Imagination Lead Us to God

Story

I was at a special preview of *The Passion of the Christ* that was held in the fall of 2003 for those of us in the two houses of formation the Legion had in New York State and Connecticut.

It was a nice rendition of that moment of Jesus' life, but overall it seemed a little inadequate. From my reading of Scripture, my prayer, and my viewing of the Shroud of Turin, I had a much bloodier image. I often imagine zooming in and seeing the bugs drink blood from these gaping wounds and Jesus holding back his divine power to stop them. Gibson later confirmed that they just couldn't artistically fit all the wounds from the Shroud into the movie.[95]

---

95 Cf. Jenny Cooney Carrillo, "Gibson, Mel - The Passion of the Christ: The Passion of Mel," Urban Cinefile: The World of Film in Australia - on the Internet, February 26, 2004, https://web.archive.org/web/20201001055442/https://www.urbancinefile.com.au/home/view.asp?a=8559&s=Interviews.

I was surprised that so many of my fellow seminarians said they had never visualized Jesus' passion as being so brutal. My imagination had made it far more real than even the movie could.

When I watched *The Passion* a second time, I appreciated the choreography in certain elements like the falls. Every year during Lent we have the option of rewatching it, but I find I already have a more amazing version of the Passion in my imagination, so I usually skip it.

Passage

O taste and see that the LORD is good!
Blessed is the man who takes refuge in him! (Ps 34:8)

Reflection

Jesus gives us so many ways to be aware of him and to thank him. He gives us the smell of roses, the taste of fresh blueberries, the touch of a border collie's fur, the proprioception[96] of a rocking chair, the sound of a morning birdsong, and innumerable images to lead us to him.

Everything in this world is created by him in one constant act of creation. He sustains everything from the Sequoia to the microbes we need a microscope to see. He gives us our senses to experience all these things.

Obviously, autistic senses are processed differently, which often leads to more intense experiences. Some of those are

---

96 Proprioception is the awareness of the position of the parts of and movement of our body. It is generally considered part of the sense of touch: often touch is split into several senses, including this. This is related to "vestibular stimming" that is mentioned in meditation no. 18.

unpleasant—for example, I can't stand the texture of kale or stringy meats—however, these allow us to sense some extra beauty in creation. If our hearing is sensitive, we can hear the details of the morning birdsong; if our taste is sensitive, we can notice even a slight change like using fresh, as opposed to dried, spices; if our sight is sensitive, we can see the intensity of different colors in paintings or flowers. Even if we are hyposensitive, that too can be a mode to sense other things like noticing differences in something so bright that others assume it is just pure light.

Whatever we sense with the external senses is what feeds our imagination. Our imagination is an inner sense where we taste and see the Lord internally, in what we imagine. All of this can help lead us to God through what we sense or what we imagine. God gave us these faculties to recognize the beauty in this world and lead us to him.

Prayer

Lord, you created this whole world, inspired the saints, and gave us the Bible—all so we would have a plethora of things to sense and imagine while leading us to you. Help me come to you through them.

26. Seeing Particulars First

Story

If you ask me to think of a Bible verse, hundreds run through my head, among them: John 1:1, Genesis 3:15, Isaiah 53:3, Revelation 1:13. I see them written in various fonts, in older or newer Bibles, on websites, or in sermons.

I've come to realize this is far from how most people think: they either remember a vague idea of a Bible verse, or their favorite verse like John 3:16. They don't instantly recall twenty or two hundred. Even if you say John 3:16 to me, I'll remember it in a few different Bibles where I read it; I'll remember a sermon on it; I'll remember looking it up to compare translations on an online reference site; I'll remember Tim Tebow wearing it in his eye black, and the fact that on that day "John 3:16" became a number one Google-search topic, and so forth.

Most of us have a very detailed memory that helps us to navigate the world. However, in its actual detail, we can often run into problems with generalization. As an adult, I've slowly learned to give less and less detail in summaries because people have told me many times that I've given too much detail.

Thus, our memory is a gift from God, but it is also a struggle. We can be very detailed but sometimes too much so.

Passage

"Even the hairs of your head are all numbered" (Mt 10:30).

Reflection

This verse is found a passage about not worrying and most commentaries view it in that light. They view it as if numbering your hairs is just a vague idea of Providence. However, it also teaches us that in certain ways God's mind corresponds to an autistic mind: he has counted everything out perfectly because he knows everything, not just in general.

God knows every particular, like we might. When we see all the particulars, we need to think of how God looks on each particular with love because everything he creates, he loves into existence. Even every aspect of our life, he loves into existence.

However, such a memory also teaches us that we need to avoid certain things like horror movies or pornography, since we will never forget them. I have had to avoid movies because of this: I remember when people much younger could handle *The Exorcism of Emily Rose*, but I could not.

God doesn't give us a gift like this without giving it to us for some task he wants us to do—whether that is programming a new surgery robot, analyzing every cooking recipe ever made, or memorizing the Bible. It is like radioactive uranium: it can power a city if used wisely or blow that city up if used unwisely.

Prayer

Jesus, thank you for my memory that is so detailed. Help me to use it to become more like you. Let my memory be yours and filled with all the good things you bring into this world. At the same time, let me see how all this reflects your glory. Amen.

27. Beyond Just Emotions

Story

I remember that once, as I was starting to take my faith seriously as a teenager, I asked my mom to drive me to what I heard was the best youth Mass in the city, taking place quite a distance from our house. So, we got to the church and before Mass they rehearsed the songs. As soon as the opening hymn started, a bunch of hands went up and people were swaying; the lyrics and the actions put emotions front and center.

I immediately felt uncomfortable. I've never been one to show my emotions publicly, and I generally follow the logic of my brain over my emotions. The whole Mass felt awkward. I didn't go back. I did realize, however, that this is probably a good way to help many teens, so this is about me fitting in, not the program being bad. At the same time, I made a prayer corner in my room with my Bible, some prayer books, and some statues. I would go there and feel close to God—my first real experiences of deeper prayer. There was some emotion in the connection I made there, but it was ultimately a connection deeper than emotions.

Passage

"Be still, and know that I am God. I am exalted among the nations, I am exalted in the earth!" (Ps 46:10)

Reflection

So often, prayer is presented in emotional terms. Beyond saying the basic prayers, such as the Our Father and Hail Mary, there seems to be a focus on the emotional aspects of prayer. Prayer is presented as a means to connect emotionally with Jesus.

Some extreme forms can be seen in certain contemporary Christian music, which critics say sounds like the artist could replace "Jesus" with the name of a romantic interest. Even more mundane forms can be found in many ministries, especially in some parish youth groups. We should have an emotional connection with God, but it should not be *only* emotional, and for many of us on the spectrum, we don't want it to be *primarily* emotional.

We need to dig deeper to find a solid foundation for our relationship with Jesus. Dr. Lamar Hardwick notes, "Most people are subconsciously afraid of digging too deep. Our culture has taught us to remain superficial."[97] It is tough to go deep with Jesus on all levels. All of us will discover unpleasant things. We might discover an attachment to sin or a behavior that is unvirtuous when we look beyond the superficial politeness.

However, when we remain still before God, when we open ourselves deeply to him and let him touch every aspect of our life, we can be transformed, we can become a saint. That is why such a deep relationship beyond only emotions matters.

Prayer

Jesus, you know me at every point, in every respect. Help me go deeper in my relationship with you: reveal what I need to change to become more like you.

28. Praying for Others

Story

Gladys Feighan was pleasantly surprised to hear that Father Solanus Casey, in his last days, had been transferred to a hospital she happened to be visiting. He'd spent years in New York and Detroit, where he had built up a reputation as a holy priest. Gladys was struggling with pregnancies: her last three pregnancies had resulted in miscarriages or babies born dead due to a genetic blood issue. A friend of hers had received healing from Father Solanus' prayers, so she wanted his prayers too.

---

97 Hardwick, *I Am Strong*, 71.

She went and asked the brother watching Father Solanus for a minute to ask the dying priest for prayers. Father Solanus was always generous about seeing people who were asking for prayers, so he accepted this request too. Father Solanus asked, "What, Gladys, do you want from God?"

She replied, "I want a baby. Another baby."

"A baby! For a woman to want a baby—how blessed. To hold God's own creation in your own hands."

Gladys explained all her health issues and Father Solanus assured her that she wasn't being selfish. He replied, "Just have confidence in our dear Lord's infinite love. . . . You will have another child, Gladys. Your Blessed Mother will give you another child." A few years later, Gladys had healthy twins.[98]

Passage

Pray at all times in the Spirit, with all prayer and supplication. To that end keep alert with all perseverance, making supplication for all the saints (Eph 6:18).

Reflection

When we first start praying, we often think of it as some basic prayers along with mentioning that we are praying for the remission of grandma's cancer and for our test tomorrow at school. As we advance, we can devalue this type of prayer. We can think we

---

[98] This story is adapted from Patricia Treece, "The Many Miracles of Solanus Casey," Catholic Exchange, November 14, 2017, https://catholicexchange.com/many-miracles-solanus-casey.

should focus on praise, intercession, and thanksgiving, moving petition to a secondary place.

However, as we read the Bible, we see numerous passages where intercessory prayer is narrated as a good act. At other times it is encouraged, as in the passage above from Saint Paul. God wants that to be part of our prayer. We come to him as we are. This should include coming to him as needy people, as people who need his grace for ourselves and others. This should lead to intercessory prayer. In this sense, intercessory prayer is a form of humility, admitting that we rely on God, admitting that we can't take care of these things ourselves. Spiritual authors often put humility as one of the most important virtues to grow in spiritually. It is one of the rarest virtues in the people I've met.

Saint Paul suggests that not only should we pray for others, but we should persevere and keep praying for them. In Greek, holy ones and saints are the same word, and Saint Paul uses this term to refer to all Christians in the family of God. Thus, in that passage he wants all of us to pray for each other.

Prayer

Lord, you know everything, you know what I need, but I still ask you to help me and my family with what we need.

29. Mystical Contemplation

Story

On the *Wrong Planet* discussion boards I found two comments on autistic prayer that apply to mystical contemplation.

Leejosepho stated, "I think 'prayer' is a lot like being 'on frequency' with supernatural things—kind of like having a radio turned on—but then things after that are dependent upon whether or not I want to actually participate within the spiritual realm. I can, of course, just 'listen in' and learn some things from that, or I can also 'interact' if I wish and listen for response."

Unduki replied, "When you pray, it's just God. You leave yourself behind bit by bit and enter the inner sanctum (power up the CB in your private CB closet). This is where I just wait and the focus is God. That's when he tells me things. It took a lot of regular practice to be able to clear my mind, and if I stop praying for a week or more, it takes a minute to find my center again. There is a physical feeling that comes from deep communion with God."[99]

Contemplation, in the sense of a prayer of deep union with God, is hard to describe. It is something beyond our senses, so here is where words really fail. However, the radio analogy can be helpful, and I think it might be particularly helpful for us autistics.

Passage

> One thing have I asked of the LORD,
> that will I seek after;
> that I may dwell in the house of the LORD
> all the days of my life,
> to behold the beauty of the LORD,
> and to inquire in his temple (Ps 27:4).

---

99 "Do You Think Prayer Is Real? Your Opinion? Wrong Planet Autism Community Forum," Discussion Board, Wrong Planet, January 29, 2012, https://wrongplanet.net/forums/viewtopic.php?f=20&t=188137&start=32.

Reflection

God wants to have us close. Our heart ultimately longs for a close relationship with him. The psalmist asks the same of the Lord: that he be allowed to dwell with the Lord. Jesus wants to be with us. He wants us to be with him directly in prayer.

This union with God is something that we feel deep in our soul: deeper than our emotions, senses, or imagination. It is direct touching of God where we want to just stay there for a time. It is a protracted gaze on the Trinity in a way where God takes possession of us, causing the soul to act in a passive rather than active manner. This is not something we can achieve but is a pure gift of God. It is something he gives when he wills; however, generally he gives it to those who dedicate themselves to varied forms of prayer.

Although this is not something we can achieve, our prayer is directed towards preparing the soul to receive this gift. This gift is something beyond any pleasures of the world. When you hear of a monk or nun joyfully living a life that otherwise seems very hard, it is this union that sustains them.

Prayer

Jesus, draw me close to you. Lead me to be united with you in Spirit and Truth.

30. Coming Close to Mary

Story

Jane, an autistic woman in the United Kingdom, was a member of a small Legion of Mary group with six active members between the parish's two towns. They would go visiting houses—up to one hundred a week, leaving rosaries and miraculous medals, praying the Rosary with those they met, and inviting those who were away from Church to come back. At the group's suggestion Jane started a weekly Rosary on Fridays. She continued it when the group broke up after a priest-transfer. Slowly this praying grew from once a week to averaging about ten decades of the Rosary a day. Sometimes she even used it rather than counting sheep when struggling to sleep. She did a silent retreat where she prayed 800 decades for vocations (a little short of her 1,000-decade goal).

Jane noted how the Rosary has helped her beyond just prayer: "In times when I feel like a meltdown might be coming on, I just take my rosary out of my pocket and hold it, and if I'm in public (like at a shop or something) or around people I will pray until I feel my inner being calming. I have not had a meltdown in six months, as I've gotten better at this." Praying the Rosary even helped her get through a physical injury where she was bleeding profusely. For Jane, it is not so much a single moment but the constant presence of Mary as she prays the Rosary that helps her physically, emotionally, and spiritually.

Passage

And a great sign appeared in heaven, a woman clothed with the sun, with the moon under her feet, and on her head a crown of twelve stars; she was with child and she cried out in her pangs of birth, in anguish for delivery (Rev 12:1–2).

Reflection

Many struggle to understand why Catholics pray to Mary. I always ask Protestants: if they were sick, would they ask their pastor and church-lady grandma to pray for them? Most agree about asking others to pray for them, but they still struggle with the concept that we can also ask those on the other side of the grave.

However, we need to remember that we are all connected in the Church, the body of Christ. We can communicate with other members without speaking. Thus, we can ask any saint to pray for us.

What has been said refers to all the prayers we ask of the deceased. Mary, as the Immaculate Mother of God, can be asked for prayers all the more. She is closest to God. She is powerful, as we see in the Book of Revelation: she appears on the clouds with a crown of stars, then helps vanquish the devil. In many statues Mary is stepping on the head of the snake to remind us of the promise of Genesis 3:15 about crushing the serpent's head, which is fulfilled in the passage from Revelation where she sends the devil away. Since she is our mother and lived through the New Testament in the flesh, we should feel her close to us and ask to share her perspective.

Prayer

Mary, help me come to you; help me come to Jesus; let me become more like you.

God Helps with My Autistic Struggles

31. Caring for Myself

Story

When I first got assigned as a priest, I pushed myself extremely hard. I was working full time in a school, plus I tried to make sure I covered Masses every Sunday, prepared every homily and interaction in depth, continued to write regular blog articles, and ran a youth ministry. I wouldn't take much time off. I ended up being alone most nights for dinner.

I was burnt out. I remember that I was running on fumes. I would try to cheer myself up when it was a special day with some extra treat with dinner, or I would go for an interesting jog around town, but nothing seem to be helping. After this first year, the school didn't want me back because it seemed I was not picking up on kids' social cues. This led to my autism diagnosis, which I'm happy about, but in hindsight I realize that my burnout probably made all the notable weaknesses in those areas worse.

After that year, when I got to a more stable situation and had my diagnosis, I started to realize the need to self-care in order to avoid burnout.

Passage

If you really fulfill the royal law, according to the Scripture, "You shall love your neighbor as yourself" (Jas 2:8).

Reflection

We have probably heard the two great commandments: love God with all your heart and love your neighbor as yourself. One thing we can pass over about the second commandment is that we are to love ourselves first. This can obviously be overkill when we fail to share that love. However, I think a rule-focused Christianity can make it happen that we just keep doing for God and for others but forget ourselves to our own detriment. We autistics have two tendencies making this more likely for us: our own tendency to focus on rules, and our own sensory or executive function issues that make our self-care less automatic.

Even beyond what is noted above, I know that when I don't have a schedule for the day, I can realize at 3:00 PM that I have yet to eat lunch and only notice because I'm feeling a bit off, not because I'm directly hungry.

Autistic anxiety can be a challenge for us. A lot of it can come from the sense we often have of trying to help others and to give ourselves to them. In so doing, we give them the power over our lives, which can make us anxious as we struggle with insecurity and control. We need to find balance with those around us so that we can help them without losing our peace. As an example, I can cook a meal once or twice a week for my community, but we need to agree at the beginning of the week on which days and not just tell me at breakfast that I'm cooking dinner that night.

We need to be able to love ourselves and take care of ourselves so we don't burn out, so we can pray, so we can fulfill the mission

God has for us. This love is often expressed in self-care such as giving yourself time to read a novel or go for a walk in the park.

Prayer

Jesus, I know you love me. Help me to love myself and care for myself so I can follow you better.

32. When Sensory Overload Comes

Story

I'm not too bad with sensory overload. I tend to have a smaller range than most neurotypicals for sensory input, but that range is close enough to theirs that it usually doesn't cause issues. For example, I have the brightest room lights of anyone in my community, but I'm the first to put on sunglasses if we are outside.

Recently the new archbishop was installed where I lived. We priests arrived up to an hour and a half early. We spent that time catching up with old friends. There was chatter on every side and it was hard to distinguish the voice of the person in front of you. The procession and Mass lasted almost three hours. Where I was seated, everything was both loud and a little difficult to make out. Back in the room where we had vested there was more chatter for another thirty minutes.

Afterward I was done. I made it home but went into a kind of shutdown mode and needed most of the next day to recover. One thing I decided after this was to get some high-fidelity earplugs (earplugs that don't muffle sound) to at least keep the volume down in situations like this. I also became more aware of my own limits.

Passage

"Fear not, for I have redeemed you;
I have called you by name, you are mine.
When you pass through the waters I will be with you;
and through the rivers, they shall not overwhelm you;
when you walk through fire you shall not be burned,
and the flame shall not consume you.
For I am the LORD your God,
the Holy One of Israel, your Savior" (Is 43:1–3).

Reflection

God tells us not to be afraid. Things can seem overwhelming, but he promises that he will be with us. In the passage above, he uses the analogy of fear coming over us like water. Water can completely envelop us in a way analogous to sensory overload. Isaiah also talks about walking through flames, and that matches the experiences of sensory overload when we feel like our eyes or ears are burning.

But in these moments, God is still there. God is still protecting us, he still calls us by name, he wants us to be together. God does not promise us a magic pill to overcome the unpleasantness of sensory overload, but he promises to be with us through it, giving us the strength to get through. In our hardest moment he is there for us, even when we feel like we can't handle it.

Prayer

Jesus, help me through the moments where my senses are overloading. Stay with me and help me to keep going with you by my side.

33. A Meltdown/Shutdown Is Not the End

Story

Saint Thérèse of Lisieux was overwhelmed a lot when she was younger. She was not autistic but had an attachment issue after her mother's death. If she woke and did not see one of her older sisters or her dad, she would cry. In her retreat before First Communion at age eleven, she cried when someone combed her hair differently from how her sister did at home. A single wrong word in catechism class would also make her cry.

She then had two experiences that helped her out of this. The first was when she received Communion for the second time and felt the ineffable sweetness of Jesus' presence in her life: his first kiss.

Later, she had a conversion experience at Christmas in 1886. She was nearly overwhelmed by emotion when her father mentioned with slight irritation that this would be the last year she'd have a childish Christmas. Up to this point, such a comment would have sent her into a flood of tears, but God gave her the grace to overcome it. This seems like an extraordinary grace, as she in no way had willed this change. We may never be able to completely overcome a meltdown, but Jesus is present with us in those just like he was present to Thérèse.

Passage

We have this treasure in earthen vessels, to show that the transcendent power belongs to God and not to us. We are afflicted in every way, but not crushed; perplexed, but not driven to despair (2 Cor 4:7–8).

Reflection

Sometimes sensory overload goes too far and we shut down or meltdown. We can't take it anymore. This is a horrible experience that we try to avoid: we can think it is the end. However, it is not all over.

Meltdowns or shutdowns happen in autistics as a response to sensory overload; unpredictability, causing executive functioning troubles; anxiety; social issues; and more. We need time to recover. This is all a normal reaction to our body getting too much. It is similar to other natural reactions necessary to maintain a healthy equilibrium, such as sweating or vomiting. These reactions aren't moral or immoral in themselves. As we get to know our bodies, we become able to foresee and avoid negative reactions. When I was eight, for example, I would eat ice cream until I was sick. Now, even though the eating part might be enjoyable, I stop at a scoop or two because I realize the bodily reaction to eating too much won't be good.

Although we autistics must deal with them often, a meltdown, like vomiting, while not a fun experience, does clear out what's wrong. We need to turn to Jesus in these moments. He is the treasure inside these earthen vessels that are prone to meltdowns. We are fragile but because he is with us, this is not the end; we can be crushed or perplexed but he will stay with us through it all. We need to turn to Jesus for strength in these hard moments.

Prayer

Jesus, be with me when I struggle the most. Let my meltdowns or shutdowns not be the end but another moment to draw closer to you.

34. Dealing with Social Situations

Story

There was a girl I went to high school and college with who clearly liked me for a long time, but it took me forever to figure that out. I never picked up on it in high school, although in hindsight I'm almost sure it was there. In one of my first classes at the local state college, she chose to sit right beside me. I still figured she was just being friendly or wanted to be with someone who went to the same high school. There were probably a whole bunch of other signs, but the first time I realized that she had feelings for me happened one day in the cafeteria. She had been eating with others, but she picked up her food and came over to sit right beside me. She started complimenting me a lot and asking me personal, but not rude, questions. I didn't ask her out right away: I lacked the courage and had promised myself no dating till the end of second year. However, I stayed close to her for a bit, and then just before I was ready to ask her out formally, I received the call to be a priest.

Passage

But Peter said, "Man, I do not know what you are saying." And immediately, while he was still speaking, the cock crowed. And the Lord turned and looked at Peter. And Peter remembered the word of the Lord, how he had said to him, "Before the cock crows today, you will deny me three times" (Lk 22:60–61).

Reflection

Quinton Deeley uses the full story of Peter's denials to show how theory of mind works in the Gospels. He notes, "The guards believe that Peter does not know Jesus," but when thinking about Peter, "Peter is only pretending not to know Jesus, and really Peter knows and loves Jesus."[100] Even when reading the Gospels, we see issues with social communication: Peter knows that those gathered at the high priest's house won't look positively on him as a friend of Jesus, but he also knows that, even though he's weak, he does love Jesus.

If we think about it consciously, we can often get others' social cues. But I think all of us have situations where we have missed others' cues, as I did in the story above. Oftentimes, we can let people know we are autistic and explain that they need to be clearer in words. I know I've had to ask my religious community not to lead me down the road by pretending that something incorrect is true. For some reason neurotypicals may think of this as fun. Much of the time people close to us will make a sincere effort to accommodate us in this.

Prayer

Lord, I know I don't notice everything socially, but help me notice what matters.

---

100 Quinton Deeley, "Cognitive Style, Spirituality, and Religious Understanding: The Case of Autism," *Journal of Religion, Disability & Health* 13, no. 1 (February 3, 2009): 78, https://doi.org/10.1080/15228960802581479.

35. The Humility to Accept Misunderstanding

Story

At a conference in Rome, the head of the National Catholic Partnership on Disability shared an anonymous story of an autistic boy who was sixteen, but his mother considered him mentally only two or three. She bathed, diapered, dressed, and often fed her son. The mother said, "But his laugh lights the room and he has taught me the meaning of unconditional love, faith that there is a reason for all that comes to us, grace and the sanctity and glory of all life. Regular Mass was too much for him—the number of people, the volume of the singing, the length, the looks of disapproval for making involuntary sounds from the other parishioners . . . but we found the Adapted Liturgy at a parish in Portland, OR and we were forever changed. Once a month a special Mass is held—lights are low, singing and music are beautiful but not overwhelming, it is a small group of people—and most magically of all . . . our special loved ones can be themselves. If they speak out or yell or move strangely people smile and don't judge. We can celebrate difference and pray for strength without pity but with smiles. Garrett goes to this liturgy and SMILES—he lays his head quietly on my shoulder and just *is* and in that moment I know God is with us."[101]

---

101 Janice L. Benton, "Animating Hope in Christian Communities throughout America," in *Proceedings of the XXIX International Conference: The Person with Autism Spectrum Disorders: Animating Hope*, vol. XXIX.3, Dolentium Hominum (The Person with Autism Spectrum Disorders: Animating Hope, New Synod Hall, Vatican City: Pontifical Council for Health Care Workers, 2014), 92.

Passage

> O LORD, you have searched me and known me!
> You know when I sit down and when I rise up;
> you discern my thoughts from afar.
> You search out my path and my lying down,
> and are acquainted with all my ways (Ps 139:1–3).

Reflection

We know that God knows and understands us, but that does not guarantee that others do. One big difference is that God sees the depths of our heart while others can only see the surface. In the depths, our true selves are revealed clearly. In return, God lets us see into his depths, he allows our autistic senses to grasp him in his fullness, something which others don't often allow.

Tony Attwood, a psychologist specializing in autism, notes, "Neurotypicals usually anticipate words and gestures of compassion and affection, but the problem for those with an ASD is that these may not be their own most effective and preferred emotion repair strategies." We could just remain here and get frustrated, but we can often be better off humbly admitting that communication channels between autistics and neurotypicals have broken down.

Attwood does not see admitting communication is tough as the final result. He offers a solution where we ask "the neurotypical to clearly state his or her feelings and the depths of those feelings, and what actions would alleviate the distress; or for the person with an ASD to ask exactly what he or she can do to help the person feel better."[102] It is a way to humbly admit that our

---

[102] Tony Attwood, *Been There. Done That. Try This!: An Aspie's Guide to Life of on Earth*, ed. Craig R. Evans and Anita Lesko, 1 edition (London; Philadelphia: Jessica Kingsley Publishers, 2014), 289.

communication sometimes breaks down and thus to use other channels for what we need to communicate.

Prayer

Lord Jesus, you communicate with me better than anyone else. I want to communicate with others, but this does not always work. When it doesn't work, help me to accept this and to improve communication when I can.

36. Being the Good Samaritan

Story

Once I stopped to make my Holy Hour in a parish that I knew had an adoration chapel. For whatever reason, that day adoration was up in the main church and there were noticeably more people than usual. I slid into a back pew and started praying. About twenty minutes in, a man tapped me on my shoulder and asked to talk.

We went off to the attached parish hall and sat at a table. He had strong homosexual tendencies and admitted he was not perfect in living chastity. Part of him wanted to be chaste, but he didn't always succeed. He was considering becoming Catholic. However, when he went to Mass, he felt judged. So, instead he would go to adoration a few times a week where he felt more of a connection with Jesus.

I encouraged him to try to live chastely, and when he left he seemed intent to struggle more for virtue. Somehow, I had been able to enter into his sense of being excluded and help him. If a priest had treated him as excluded at that moment, it might have driven him from Catholicism.

Passage

"A man was going down from Jerusalem to Jericho, and he fell among robbers, who stripped him and beat him, and departed, leaving him half dead. Now by chance a priest was going down that road; and when he saw him he passed by on the other side. So likewise a Levite, when he came to the place and saw him, passed by on the other side. But a Samaritan, as he journeyed, came to where he was; and when he saw him, he had compassion, and went to him and bound up his wounds, pouring on oil and wine; then he set him on his own beast and brought him to an inn, and took care of him" (Lk 10:30–34).

Reflection

We autistics need more time to take care of our own needs. We need down time to avoid sensory overload, we need time to recover, we need time to stim alone, and so forth. But Jesus calls us all to live in charity like the Good Samaritan. How can we do this?

One thing we might note about the story of the Good Samaritan is that he can identify with the sense of being an outcast, like the man on the side of the road, in a way that the priest and Levite probably had never experienced themselves. I think the difficulties we have in life are often a great means for us to be more charitable. The experience I have had of being rejected from a friend group helps me to see how another person can be an outcast from society. This background can be particularly valuable in having charity toward other neurodiverse people. I think that being neurodiverse ourselves means that we can sympathize with them better. I find that I can understand my fellow neurodiverse people better than neurotypicals can. This provides a specific channel for charity where we can excel. Many who are neurodiverse need help, and we are better at it; also, giving such help tends to tire us less. We can be the Good Samaritan to our neurodiverse brothers and sisters in Christ, and to their families.

Prayer

Jesus, I know that you care for the excluded like myself. Help me to enter into the reality of being excluded and help others who are also excluded.

The Life of Jesus

37. Jesus as the Model of All Virtue

Story

Léonie Martin is perhaps the lesser-known sister of Saint Thérèse of Lisieux. Léonie had emotional issues as a child, regularly throwing what others called "tantrums," but which may have been meltdowns. She was gullible and a mean family maid would often beat her behind her parents' backs. She was kicked out of boarding school three times for not playing with the other girls and focusing on her own play instead. And it took her four attempts at religious life before she was accepted for profession. Léonie's journey had taken so long that by the time of her profession, Thérèse (her younger sister by about a decade) had died and her autobiography had been published.

As people have gone through Thérèse's letters, they have found many to Léonie, encouraging her to keep thinking of a religious vocation and reminding her to follow Jesus in all things. Even after all her struggles, Léonie had difficulty adapting to religious life. Her clumsiness and difficulty in changing tasks quickly caused her a lot of suffering and humiliation, but she saw this as helping her identify with Jesus. Her favorite job was being sacristan, for then she could more easily unite with Jesus. In the convent she followed the *Little Way* her little sister had pioneered. Since Thérèse was beatified and canonized in her lifetime, Léonie became the center of attention at the celebrations, but demonstrated humility like that of Jesus in dealing with this celebrity.

Passage

Have this mind among yourselves, which was in Christ Jesus, who, though he was in the form of God, did not count equality with God a thing to be grasped, but emptied himself, taking the form of a servant, being born in the likeness of men (Phil 2:5–7).

Reflection

This passage is often quoted starting with "Christ Jesus," indicating that it was one of the first Christian creeds. This is a valuable citation. However, we also need to remember that Saint Paul is instructing Christians to have the mind of Jesus. It is not just that we believe in an abstract way, but that we take on Jesus' mind.

Taking on Jesus' mind means practicing his virtues. When I started taking my faith seriously in the 1990s, the cool Christian phrase was WWJD, which people had on bracelets or other clothing. In my first passport photo in 2001, I'm wearing a black rope necklace with silver WWJD beads. Sure, a lot of that stuff was tacky, but the message behind it is valuable. If we ask, "What Would Jesus Do?" we put on the mind of Christ. We are able to see virtue not just as an abstract concept in Aristotle, but as something Jesus did or would do in a particular circumstance. As Christians, we are called to virtue beyond what human reason can reach, virtue modeled after Jesus. Along with being our God, our brother, and our friend, Jesus is our model in practicing virtue.

Prayer

Jesus, you model all virtue for me. Help me to be just a reflection of your overwhelming goodness.

38. Seeing Jesus in Bethlehem

Story

Legionaries of Christ from across the U.S.A. usually get together for a study week right after Christmas. Those of us who have responsibilities such that we don't need to be at a parish on Christmas (many of us work in schools, youth ministry, spiritual direction, and retreats) come early for Christmas. I remember one year when I was a religious brother, I was quite busy organizing the sacristy for midnight Mass. I was going hither and thither to make sure everything worked right. Mass went off without a hitch.

Then, after putting everything in the sacristy and turning off the chapel lights, I began to walk back to my room. As I moved upstairs, I felt a tug to enter the choir loft. I went in, knelt down, and entered deeply into the mystery. Everyone else had gone to bed but at this moment I felt Jesus being born in my heart. I felt a closeness to the Nativity beyond what I had before—a kind of moment alone with Jesus beyond words.

Passage

The LORD has spoken:
"Sons have I reared and brought up,

but they have rebelled against me.
The ox knows its owner,
and the donkey its master's crib;
but Israel does not know,
my people does not understand" (Is 1:2–3).

Reflection

We often think that certain elements of the Christmas story are just tradition and not from the Bible. The donkey and ox in almost every nativity set come from the passage above and the Greek version of Habakkuk 3:2, indicating that the Lord would be manifested between two animals. We can contemplate our Lord in his simplicity. He came to people who rebelled against him and didn't understand him. He came in a simple way, born amidst the animals and laid in their food trough (the manger).

I think it valuable to look at all the sensory aspects of where Jesus was born. Most likely it was either a structure attached to a house or a cave near a house where animals were kept for the night. You can imagine it rather dark: maybe Joseph has a small oil lamp. The oil lamp produces harsh contrasts among Mary, Jesus, and the animals, with one side in light and the other in complete darkness. You can see each of the animals acting normally, but then showing reverence to their creator when baby Jesus is born. You can smell the animals. You feel the manger, a rough wood or stone food trough. As Mary starts her contractions, Joseph finds the softest hay and fabric to fill it. You hear Mary and Joseph calmly discussing and getting ready for the birth in hushed tones. You can hear as Mary approaches her time: how she begins to let out the cries of a mother in labor. (This point is debated theologically: if you prefer to imagine a painless birth, you are free to do so.) You now look in the manger and there is the savior of the world, seen as a relatively normal, but precious-looking baby. You hear him cry out and see Mary hold him close to her chest.

Prayer

Jesus, help me see you born in Bethlehem. Be born in my heart.

39. Seeing Jesus in His Passion

Story

Kasandra, an autistic woman, had PTSD from testifying in court about physical abuse that happened to her at age twelve. Then, when she was in her thirties, she and her husband decided to go to court to remove the rights of their daughter's biological father so the dad she'd known her whole life could adopt her fully.

She realized she would need to testify in front of her abusive ex, and that he would also testify. Kasandra describes what went through her mind, "First, I felt frightened to see my abuser. Then I kept spiraling, mentally, at the stress of having to stand before a judge. Soon I was panicking that I lacked the faith in God's healing necessary to see him glorified, and that I would make him a fool by dissolving back into a trauma state."

Then, in her panic, she heard a quiet voice, "Why are you afraid?" She responded, "Because judges can't be trusted! They couldn't give us justice before. They don't care about right and wrong. They cannot guarantee fairness. YOU DON'T UNDERSTAND."

She then noted, "And as surely as I'm sitting here, writing this story, I saw Christ in Gethsemane in my mind and I heard the answer, 'Yes I do.' I can face the court because he did. . . . In that moment he stepped into the darkness of my loneliness, isolation, and fear, and he showed me that he had walked there before. And honestly, it set me free from that fear. It really did."

Passage

> He was despised and rejected by men;
> a man of sorrows, and acquainted with grief;
> and as one from whom men hide their faces
> he was despised, and we esteemed him not. . . .
> But he was wounded for our transgressions,
> he was bruised for our iniquities;
> upon him was the chastisement that made us whole,
> and with his stripes we are healed (Is 53:3, 5).

Reflection

Jesus is beaten, bruised, and broken. We autistics can be bruised and broken as well, but more often what we struggle with is the internal suffering. The internal suffering from PTSD, from anxiety, from sensory overload, can be overwhelming. These can often be our personal calvary.

When we go through tough moments where we are internally bruised and beaten, it is an opportunity to be with and contemplate Jesus in his passion. I think—like Kasandra—that the agony in the garden of Gethsemane is often the most poignant for us. Here Jesus takes on all the sins of the world. All the sins people committed through history are flashing through his head. Massacres and off-color jokes are passing through his head in such a quick succession that the mind can't really notice each one. He struggles. He isn't punished so much by external means like whips or nails, but by images wreaking havoc on him internally.

I think that some of us might identify more with other parts of the passion—the scourging, the way of the cross, or the crucifixion—and that in each part of the passion we can unite ourselves with Jesus' suffering.

Prayer

Jesus, you took upon yourself not only the sins of the world but my sins. In your suffering, help me through my suffering.

40. Seeing Jesus in His Resurrection

Story

Jade, an autistic woman, told me of an experience she had where she felt that Jesus was at the empty tomb. She was driving five hours north for some time of prayer and worship music with others. She was eager to get there, but because she was ahead of schedule, she felt a little tug on her heart to pull off into an elementary school parking lot.

Sitting in her car in the parking lot, she began praying silently. Then, she says, "He told me to just be quiet and be with him. I'm not sure how long we were like that, but I then saw two angels near the passenger side of the vehicle. They were beautiful beams of light. God then told me to speak and I was speaking in words that I couldn't understand. It was absolutely incredible."

Passage

Jesus said to her, "'Woman, why are you weeping? Whom do you seek?" Supposing him to be the gardener, she said to him, "Sir, if you have carried him away, tell me where you have laid him, and I will take him away." Jesus said to her, "Mary." She turned and said to him in Hebrew, "Rabboni!" (which means Teacher) (Jn 20:15–16).

Reflection

We are often like Mary Magdalene. We are close to Jesus and the joy he wants to bring, but we don't see him. We are so caught up in ourselves that we don't notice him. He might be there wanting to help us become more joyful, but we get so caught up in ourselves that we don't notice him. Maybe we're focused on our struggle with sensory input or issues with executive function, or maybe we're just so caught up in a special interest. Whatever has our mind, it is good to remind ourselves regularly of Jesus' closeness to us.

Jesus also knows us by name. Mary recognizes him when he says, "Mary." We, too, often recognize him when he says our name or talks to us in a special way we recognize. God speaks to each of us as we are, including being autistic.

We can also live the last part of this passage, where Mary Magdalene gets so excited that she screams, "Rabboni!" and grasps his feet so tightly that he asks her to let go. We should be excited about Jesus; we should cling to him. We should share our joy with him. Jesus does not just come to us in sorrow but also in joy. When we have a wonderful experience, like graduating from college or finishing a big project, it is easy to think only of ourselves. However,

Jesus is there to share our joy. He is our joy. When we start flapping uncontrollably in excitement, he flaps beside us.

Prayer

Risen Jesus, fill me with your joy: let me share the wonderful experience of the resurrection.

41. Pentecost

Story

As a child, Saint Thomas Aquinas was called "the dumb ox" because he was so quiet in class. People assumed he was not learning, but in fact he was memorizing and connecting everything. He later became one of the most prodigious theologians in the history of the Church. He wrote the *Summa Theologica*, which is still the standard for a complete theological text. As an adult he could dictate to three, or sometimes four, secretaries on different topics at the same time.

He seemed to have theology as his special interest. He would not notice when the plates were taken off the table. His confreres would invite him out to talk after eating but he would retreat to his cell alone to study theology. His memory and his ability to connect ideas were such that he wrote a commentary on the Gospels from the writings of the Fathers called the *Catena Aurea* (Golden Chain). Saint Thomas had memorized such a large number of quotations of the Fathers of the Church that he could match four volumes worth of content to specific passages of Scripture without referring to the texts themselves. I thought I had an encyclopedic autistic memory until I read about Aquinas.

At age forty-eight, he was celebrating Mass on December 6, 1273, when he had a mystical experience. He went into a prolonged ecstasy where he felt God's presence. He had had a few others in the preceding years but this one completely transformed him. After this, his secretary, Reginald, noticed he changed his routine. When asked to write more, he refused, saying, "All that I have written seems like straw." Considering that 700-plus years later what he wrote is certainly some of the most profound theology, we can only imagine what an experience of God he had.

Passage

If the Spirit of him who raised Jesus from the dead dwells in you, he who raised Christ Jesus from the dead will give life to your mortal bodies also through his Spirit who dwells in you (Rom 8:11).

Reflection

When we think of the Holy Spirit, the idea of breaking routine comes to mind. If someone tells me that he or she is a "Spirit-filled Christian," I immediately think of the charismatic renewal or Pentecostalism. However, the Holy Spirit can come into our ordinary life. The Holy Spirit inspires people not only to occasionally do extraordinary things, but regularly to do ordinary things, such as follow a daily routine.

In the passage above, Saint Paul reminds us that as Christians we always have the Holy Spirit working in us, whether we look charismatic or not. The Holy Spirit is powerful, in that he raised Jesus from the dead and will raise us on the last day. Then we go back to Aquinas: the Holy Spirit was inspiring his mind when he did his great theology while following a strict daily routine, as well as during those final days where he felt overwhelmed by God's presence and could no longer write. The Holy Spirit is with us always and will inspire us, even if his inspiration is to eat our "same food," or an inspiration to step out beyond our comfort zone.

Prayer

Holy Spirit, who inspired the apostles on Pentecost, inspire me in my daily life.

The Sacraments

42. A Sacramental Worldview

Story

Saint Thorlák Thórhallsson was a rather private, studious young man who lived in Iceland in the 1100s. In her biography of Thorlák, Aimée O'Connell has made him the patron for Autism Consecrated, based on how others described his deliberate and literal manner in relationships, and on the fact that he read and spoke like a theologian from his early childhood.

Thorlák's sister, Ragnheidh, caught the eye of the king's grandson, Jón, who was ten years her senior. Even though this boded well for his family, Thorlák was concerned—both because Jón, being older, might take advantage of his sister and because it seemed unlikely that the two would ever marry. Eventually Jón entered a politically advantageous marriage, but kept Ragnheidh as his mistress. In the Iceland of that time, having a mistress was normal for a powerful chieftain or prince. Marriage was considered more as a contract between families, and not really a sacrament, even though the Icelanders had formally embraced

Christianity. Thorlák, who by now had been ordained a priest, took issue with the illicit relationship of Jón and Ragnheidh.

Eventually Jón became the most powerful chieftain in Iceland, and through his political machinations and Thorlák's humility, the earnest priest found himself appointed successor to the bishop. However, Jón got something he did not expect when Thorlák made a strong case for sacramental marriage. Formal recognition of Jón's marriage as a sacrament would call for the resolution of Ragnheidh's situation as mistress.

Thorlák spoke to his sister directly, reminding her of God's love and noting, "I have watched you waste your entire life waiting to be loved by someone who will never love you!"[103] The two siblings embraced. Then Thorlák spoke to Jón, who claimed that Ragnheidh was the only one who really loved him. Thorlák responded that God had loved him first. Jón and Ragnheidh's son, who was a priest under Thorlák, told his father he should not leave Ragnheidh in such a situation. So Jón found an honorable widower for her to marry and renounced her as his mistress.

Passage

The LORD God formed man of dust from the ground, and breathed into his nostrils the breath of life; and man became a living soul (Gen 2:7).

Reflection

There are three fundamental ways to view the world: there is just the material world; there are separate and distinct spiritual

---

103 O'Connell, Aimée, *Thorlák of Iceland: Who Rose Above Autism to Become Patron Saint of His People* (San Jose, CA: Chaos to Order Publishing, 2018), 210.

and material worlds; there is an interpenetration of the spiritual and physical worlds. The second account of creation in Genesis, noted above, clearly sets the Christian worldview as the third. God creates us as embodied spirits. He breathes a breath into us that animates both body and soul.

What this means is that our physical actions have spiritual meaning. A real change happens when two people go before a priest and their family and friends and say, "I, [name], take you, [name], to be my wife/husband. I promise to be faithful to you, in good times and in bad, in sickness and in health, to love you and to honor you all the days of my life."[104] Physical actions have spiritual meanings. Our spiritual life is not separate from our physical life, but they are intertwined.

This is called the "sacramental worldview," since the sacraments are where this intertwining is clearest. However, intertwining goes deeper. When I sin, I break a real union with God. When I repent, grace transforms me from within: it does not just cover me with snow, leaving a completely broken human nature underneath (Luther's view). Every action we perform can thus lead us in the life of sin or the life of grace.

Prayer

Jesus, I know you make me, body and soul united: help me to see this and cooperate with your action.

---

104 USCCB, "The Exchange of Consent," from the Rite of Celebrating Matrimony, copyright © United States Conference of Catholic Bishops, https://www.foryourmarriage.org/the-marriage-vows/.

43. Our Baptism Changes Us

Story

I was baptized two weeks after I was born. Although I have a good memory, the only proof I have are the words of my parents and godparents and a few photos of the ceremony. On the other hand, my first nephew was born soon after I became a deacon, so his was the first baptism I did.

I remember it well, as I was new to it and was trying to make sure I didn't mess things up. One of my other sisters and her husband were the godparents, so it was a whole family affair. This sister, the baby's mother, wanted the baptism to be by immersion, not just the pouring, which is standard in infant baptism, so the more experienced deacon gave me complete instructions on how to do that safely—I started worrying that I'd drop him in the water and he'd half-drown. In the end, everything went off without a hitch and he ended up serving when I baptized his little brother five years later. Watching him grow up, I can really see grace at work. He is growing up as a good Christian.

Passage

We were buried therefore with him by baptism into death, so that as Christ was raised from the dead by the glory of the Father, we too might walk in newness of life. For if we have been united with him in a death like his, we shall certainly be united with him in a resurrection like his (Rom 6:4–5).

Reflection

As autistics, we tend to be sensitive to changes. We might like slight variation but within the same structure. Baptism gives us a Christian structure to our lives. It is possible to receive grace and even be saved while not formally embracing Christianity. However, Baptism gives us a regularity of grace and a promise of salvation in the spiritual realm much like what we seek in the physical realm.

Saint Paul reminds us that in Baptism, we united our life with Jesus. We die with him so we can rise with him and live in the newness of life. Living in this new life does not make us unautistic, but it gives us a peace in how we live as autistics. As we are made part of the household of God, we can live in a way that is peaceful and ideal for us.

Baptism gives us the comfort of knowing that God is always near, that we can always talk to him. It makes our life a constant life of grace. It gives a kind of gentle, pleasant background noise to our life.

Prayer

Lord, who was baptized by John and entrusted Baptism to your apostles, help me to see the value of my Baptism.

44. The Liturgy as a Schedule for Worshiping God

Story

When I was in college, a Franklin Graham rally was coming to town. It was ecumenical, so I decided to participate as one of the people helping those who had come to the altar to return to whatever Christian church they were familiar with, or to my church (Catholic, obviously) if they weren't familiar with any church.

For the teens and young adults, the training was at a local independent evangelical church named after the street it was on. It had this large sanctuary with plush chairs. They started with a worship song or two, then they spoke a little bit of training, then another worship song, then more explanation, and so forth. They obviously had a plan, but as an autistic Catholic I felt very uncomfortable. I had no idea what was coming next. Other than the obvious progression of the training, there seemed to be no order. This helped me appreciate how when I go to Mass each day, I have a kind of schedule that I know will be followed. After the readings comes the homily, then the offertory, then the Eucharistic Prayer, then the Our Father and then Communion, just as it was described in the Didache in the first century.

Passage

He has made everything beautiful in its time; also he has put eternity into man's mind, yet so that he cannot find out what God has done from the beginning to the end. I know that there is nothing better for them than to be happy and enjoy themselves as long as they live (Eccles 3:11–12).

Reflection

I think the repeating structure of liturgy is helpful to everyone. First, because this is how God has asked us to worship, and second because it gives us a sense of what is next. For us autistics I think it takes on a whole different level of importance, due to our issues with sensory overload and executive functioning.

I can see how a lot of contemporary-style Protestant worship services with rock bands and lighting effects, among other things, can be a huge cause of sensory overload. Fortunately for us, most Catholic churches are not like this during Sunday Mass. Some events like youth conferences might go this direction, but we have plenty of warning to decide if we will go and what means we put into place to avoid a shutdown or meltdown. The forced social interaction in some churches can also cause similar effects. However, one can sit alone in a Catholic church and nod to others at the sign of peace.

Executive functioning can also be a big problem when we don't know what is coming. Some of us have such trouble with this that we need everything the same. I, at least, don't need everything exactly the same, but if you make a change with less than forty-eight hours' notice I don't take it well. Having a set schedule in the liturgy can be a big help for us.

The author of Ecclesiastes reminds us that God made each thing at the right time for it. At Mass we experience God's infinity, but in a way we can comprehend. The liturgy is that which we can enjoy from now till the end of time.

Prayer

Jesus, you come to me regularly through the liturgy. Help me to see you there.

45. Seeing Jesus in the Eucharist

Story

Catherine, an autistic woman, still remembers receiving Communion on her wedding day and the Sunday after as experiences of prayer that have remained with her. She explains, "It's these first of many Communions that are the closest I will be to my husband and reality this side of the veil." She noted how the Eucharist after marriage made her feel closer to both her husband and Jesus. She continues, "I felt it; I was not alone, I was where I should be, I was who I should be, I was loved. I actually felt reality, at least for a few moments."

She noted that the wedding itself was a disaster and didn't go off like a fairytale wedding. The priest who officiated was later accused of pedophilia. The family toasts didn't go smoothly, and Catherine felt insulted by her father. The food did not work out. Her homemade veil didn't work. Catherine had endometriosis flaring up that day on top of some regular physical difficulties she deals with. There was a slip, and someone almost cut off a finger with the cake knife.

Despite what might seem like a disaster, overall, Catherine notes that this was a positive experience. She concludes, "I was given a glimpse of who I really was."

Passage

For as often as you eat this bread and drink the chalice, you proclaim the Lord's death until he comes (1 Cor 11:26).

Reflection

The Eucharist is a complete transformation. We are united to Jesus sacramentally. Jesus is close to us as a friend and saves us. We are with him awaiting his second coming. Although the Eucharist looks and tastes like bread, in order to see him there, we need to remember that this is Jesus.

One thing about this union is that since God comes to us in accord with our autistic manner, we can visualize this however we want. Often people think of it as Jesus inside of them or Jesus hugging them, but this does not always work for an autistic. We can visualize Jesus beside us chatting about our special interest or speaking kind words to us quietly. Jesus unites himself to us in a way we can understand, in a way that will conform to us as autistics. Jesus is really there for us.

The Eucharist is our food. So often we can have a limited number of foods that we eat over and over. I know I eat the same thing two meals a day in most cases. The Eucharist can be one of those "same foods" that gives us comfort. It not only can give us physical comfort like other same foods but can also give us spiritual comfort, for we know we are strongly united with Jesus.

Prayer

Jesus, who became man and then became bread to unite yourself with me, help me to appreciate your gift of the Eucharist.

46. The Father of Mercies in Confession

Story

Jake, a 36-year-old married autistic man, was once on retreat where there was a reconciliation service with a group of priests. The priests were stationed around the edge of the church, while the retreatants sat in the middle waiting for any priest to be free or for the priest they wanted to confess with to be available.

Jake notes, "I remember sitting in the pews while people were going to all the priests for reconciliation. I prayed for those going to reconciliation and gave gratitude to God as I examined my conscience. I was immediately overwhelmed with excitement and awe and then began sobbing uncontrollably at the overwhelming feeling of love that I felt God had for everyone present, and I 'knew'/ felt the presence of our Lord more than other times."

Jake usually goes to confession every month, but felt a much stronger experience of God's presence that day.

Passage

Is any among you sick? Let him call for the elders of the Church, and let them pray over him, anointing him with oil in the name of the Lord; and the prayer of faith will save the sick man, and the Lord will raise him up; and if he has committed sins, he will be forgiven (Jas 5:14–15).

Reflection

We can ask: "Why confess to a priest rather than just to God?" This is a legitimate question. The reality is that going back right to apostolic times, there was a clear belief that a special blessing, which we now call absolution, could be granted by a priest, but not by another. In the letter of Saint James above, the word "elder" is actually "presbyter," which is another term for "priest." In English, we don't use this term much except to refer to all the priests of a diocese as the presbyterate. Nonetheless, Saint James thinks that a priest can give a special blessing that can forgive sins.

As autistics, we often struggle to go to confession. It is a social interaction after all. We can also tend toward scruples. We need to realize that certain things we might do—like saying something inappropriate or misreading someone's emotions—are not sins if done unintentionally.

In the confessional, we struggle more. Be honest with the priest about being autistic. If you struggle with eye contact, just use the screen so you don't even have to think about that. If you are nervous, realize that is normal and don't fret. If you are unable to say your sins, using AAC (Augmentative and Alternative Communication—a way for non-verbal autistics to communicate) or writing them out is acceptable. The person must communicate his or her sins to the priest, and although speaking is the most common way, it is not the only way. (If using other methods, try to prevent disclosure by burning the paper you wrote on or clearing the AAC for that period.)

Hopefully, these tips can help you to have a fruitful autistic confession. For further information, please see Appendix D on page 207.

Prayer

Lord, you know how I struggle with confession. Help me make a good confession.

47. Accepting God's Mercy

Story

Saint Christina the Astonishing is known for her amazing miracles. However, for most of her adult life she lived in a convent, shunning the presence of others and only responding to the prioress (head nun) of the convent. She would also do things that others thought strange, such as spin, roll in a ball to pray, or seem insensitive to some sense inputs while being hyper-sensitive to others.

Her life had been normal until she reached her early twenties, when she had a massive seizure and was assumed dead. At her funeral, she stood up in her coffin, then flew from everyone to the rafters of the Church, noting how sinful they all were. In the time between the seizure and funeral, Christina was given an amazing vision of the sufferings of hell and purgatory. The fact that she was saved from that and also could help save others, led her to live the rest of her life in extreme penance. She wore rags and lived in desolate conditions. She even endured what would seem like inhuman tortures, such as going into fire or into freezing water, then through a water wheel with no indication of any serious or permanent damage to her body. Her stories seem incredible, but we have these in contemporary reports from bishops, not legends written down decades or centuries later.

Passage

> Bless the LORD, O my soul, and forget not all his benefits,
> who forgives all your iniquity, who heals all your diseases,
> who redeems your life from the Pit,
> who crowns you with mercy and compassion (Ps 103:2–4).

Reflection

God forgives everything. It is easy to consider his mercy as only partial. That is why the psalmist invites us to forget not God's benefits, including his forgiveness of all our iniquities. God doesn't sit there measuring his mercy drop by drop. Instead, he pours it abundantly on the Christian who will accept it.

We autistics must often measure how much we give to others: we need to foresee things and plan well, so our commitment to others is often more quantified and less spontaneous than that of most neurotypicals. I know that I need to consider a lot more factors when saying yes to a social engagement than other priests in my community. I can't just commit without info—nor at the last moment. This measuring of our commitment to certain things is required self-care for many of us. But God is just the opposite: he spreads out his mercy without measure.

I think our tendency to need to measure such things, or to be cautious when someone seems to offer us something free in order to manipulate us, means that we can be slow in accepting God's mercy. Instead, we can look at the cross or the resurrected Lord and be grateful for the amazing gift he gives us. We can bask in his mercy: I often imagine it like the vacation ads where the couple is basking in a pond while a beautiful waterfall showers upon them. In a similar way, God's mercy is a constant stream on us if we let it penetrate our soul.

Prayer

Jesus, unending font of mercy, please help me to accept and embrace your mercy.

Fighting to the End

48. Remain Watchful in Our Own Lives

Story

One of my habits is to go on long bicycle rides. The big challenge for amateur cyclists is to do one hundred miles in five hours. On relatively flat ground, I can hold 20 mph for an hour and can do a hundred miles. However, I'm still far from that goal. Once, I started a ride where I hoped I could get my time down to five hours and thirty minutes but only reached five and forty. Those long rides require a constant, continuous pushing at the limit of what we can do. Air resistance is a huge part of the effort, so cycling difficulty goes up exponentially, not linearly, with speed. For a ride like that, you don't want to blow off on a tear then relax, but keep a constant, relatively high speed. For five and thirty, I needed to maintain 18.2 mph (29.3 km/h) and I did for the first half or so of the ride, but later I slowed a bit and so averaged 17.6 mph (28.4 km/h) overall.

That constant pushing, that constant vigilance, resembles how we need to keep pushing in this life. I need to be watchful for sins I know I can easily fall into, I need to push myself to get to bed so

I get a good night's sleep, or to get up at a reasonable hour if I didn't get to bed on time. (My biggest issue here is that my mind can still be racing and I need to calm it down to be able to get into bed: turning off electronics and saying a few prayers near bedtime is often the best for me.) An endurance race is a good analogy, for the Christian life is a marathon, not a sprint.

Passage

"Then the kingdom of heaven shall be compared to ten maidens who took their lamps and went to meet the bridegroom. Five of them were foolish, and five were wise. For when the foolish took their lamps, they took no oil with them; but the wise took flasks of oil with their lamps" (Mt 25:1–4).

Reflection

In the parable of the ten maidens—which some other translations call the ten virgins—we see two groups of people. One doesn't plan at all, not bringing any extra lamp oil; the other considers other possibilities, bringing sufficient lamp oil to last the night. Although in other places, Jesus praises those who live in the moment, here he praises the ones who bring extra lamp oil. In fact, the very phrasing of them at the beginning as the "wise" and "foolish" indicates Jesus' editorial line pretty well.

In our own lives, we often bring more things with us than other people do. We often must bring stim toys or weighted blankets when others don't. In doing so we are like the wise maidens, providing whatever we will need. We also must be wise and prudent in other ways, in order to know when we need to put in tons of effort to read others' emotions or when we've had enough and need a break. Fortitude and prudence are important virtues that should work in harmony, not in opposition.

Prayer

Jesus, help me keep moving toward you for my whole life.

49. Death

Story

The night after I finished my last exam for my second year of theology, I had a dinner celebrating work I'd done during the year translating some Regnum Christi documents into English. Then at some early hour, I was awakened by flashing lights in my room. I was told to call my brother-in-law. I got on the phone and called. It turns out my mom had had a brain aneurysm. This is serious, since these often result in death. But it looked like mom had cleared the first obstacle already because she had gotten to the hospital alive.

I had to figure out how to get on the next plane to Canada from Rome. It was a little crazy. I had to use someone else's credit card, so they flagged me at the airport for possible fraud for buying a ticket on such short notice. I rushed through everything in the morning, then got on an early plane, not knowing how long I would be gone and if mom would be alive when I got home. The first flight was a short connector to Frankfurt, and it was not too full. As soon as our airplane door closed and I was alone with my thoughts, I started crying, bawling. In fact, I cannot think of any other moment in my life when I cried so hard. It was dramatic to think of my mom possibly dying at any moment.

Although she was touch-and-go for two weeks, fortunately, my mom was in the top 20-25 percent, having no serious long-term damage. Dad says that he notices differences, but I remind him that if even my sister (who lives next door and has known mom for thirty-plus years) doesn't notice anything, it isn't too serious.

Passage

Then Jesus, crying with a loud voice, said, "Father, into your hands I commit my spirit!" And having said this he breathed his last. Now when the centurion saw what had taken place, he praised God, and said, "Certainly this man was innocent!" (Lk 23:46–47)

Reflection

Jesus was the most innocent man ever to come to earth. He and his mom were the only humans never to commit a venial sin. Yet, at the end of his life we hear him call out in agony, commending himself into the Father's hands. Death is never easy.

We need to prepare for death, because at death we all are judged to heaven, hell, or—probably most of us—to purgatory. That judgment is based on how we responded to God's grace in our lives. We can see an initial judgment in the centurion's proclamation of Jesus' innocence.

Different practices have arisen in Christian tradition for remembering our death and preparing for it. Our death is not the end but the beginning of our eternal life. You might want to adopt one practice or another: none are needed but many are possible. The goal is to remember how we have responded to grace and how we can better respond to grace in the future. Obviously, we respond to grace as autistic individuals, and it is important to remember that although we often respond differently than others do, this is not wrong. We are judged only on our choices, not about things we couldn't control.

Prayer

Jesus, I know death was hard even for you. Help me prepare for and accept my death.

50. The Resurrection: A World Without Social Disability

Story

As a teenager, I was a bit of a Trekkie. I had a friend who was much more hardcore: we went to the new Star Trek movie on opening night, and he cosplayed as a Next Generation officer (think Captain Picard minus the bald head), while I was just wearing jeans and a polo shirt. At the same time, I think Star Trek offered some insights. Often, the situations that the character Data would get into would remind me of circumstances I had been in. I was not exactly like this humanoid robot, but somehow, we ended up in similar situations.

This identification with a robotic character was not overwhelming for me, but another autistic author noted a trend: "In what has until relatively recently been a glaring absence of overt autistic representation—both real and fictional—it's no accident that many autistic people have found resonance in portrayals of artificial humans and electronic beings. Our own—more subtle—technology use forms bonds and becomes the subject of self-deprecating jokes. But the links to our autism aren't always clearly drawn. I feel technology—both the idea of using technology, and the idea of, on some level, being technology—is a crucial part of any understanding of autistic culture, but no aspect of this discussion is easy to define."[105]

Passage

Not all flesh is alike, but there is one kind for men, another for animals, another for birds, and another for fish. . . . So is it with the resurrection of the dead. What is sown is perishable, what is raised is imperishable (1 Cor 15:39,42).

Reflection

The resurrection of life is what we ultimately await. We are not sitting awaiting a kind of bodiless heaven, but our autistic bodies will be somehow transformed for the resurrection of the body at the end of time when Jesus comes again.

One of the struggles many of us recognize with our bodies in this pre-resurrected state is that we wrestle often with social disability, where it is not our body but the structures around us that create a disability. For example, having loud noises in certain places or requiring eye contact to prove honesty are not necessary for humans, but if they are required, they often create a social disability for us. In the resurrection we will still be autistic, but given the perfect knowledge of others, such social disabilities will dissipate.

---

105 A. C. Buchanan, "Cyborgs, Luddites and To-Do List Apps: An Autistic Use of Technology," in *Knowing Why: Adult-Diagnosed Autistic People on Life and Autism*, ed. Elizabeth Bartmess (Washington, DC: The Autistic Press, 2018), 139.

Bethany McKinney Fox makes a similar note about Jesus' healing miracles in a book on the theology of disability:

> Since interpreters from a disability perspective emphasize the social reality of people with illness and disability and their frequent exclusion from the domestic, religious, and social life of the community, they keenly notice aspects of the healing narratives that point to the healed person's inclusion into the community after they are healed. Inclusion, incorporation, and liberation are repeated themes as these interpreters read the narratives. Several use the adjective 'full' to describe the person's ability to participate in the community after they are healed.[106]

She also notes that today Christians often fail in this regard and mandate a certain bodily conformity that exacerbates social disability.

Prayer

Jesus, show me the joy and glory of the resurrection. Let me see the world to come where social disability is no more.

---

106 Bethany McKinney Fox, *Disability and the Way of Jesus: Holistic Healing in the Gospels and the Church* (Downers Grove, IL: IVP Academic, 2019), 89.

Go Forth Autistically

51. The Autistic Disciple

Story

Amanda, a young autistic woman diagnosed later in life, speaks of trying to share the faith with others. She sees sharing Christianity as a gift: "I walk into a room and give someone an invisible gift. They look at me askance. They can see I am trying to give them something. But they cannot see what it is I am trying to give them. They wave it to one side as in "What is this?" I try to give it to them again. They wave it to one side, getting more confused and more embarrassed as clearly I am attempting to give them something, but they cannot work out what the gift is or how to receive it. I try again. They wave it to one side again, even more agitated because they are clearly not getting the picture." This is a struggle we often have with group prayers or with sharing our faith with others where we try to offer a gift, but others don't understand. God wants us to keep sharing our faith with others even if they don't fully get it.

Passage

"Go therefore and make disciples of all nations, baptizing them in the name of the Father and of the Son and of the Holy Spirit, teaching them to observe all that I have commanded you; and behold, I am with you always, to the close of the age" (Mt 28:19–20—last verses of the Gospel).

Reflection

Every Christian is called to be a disciple: to follow Jesus, to lead others to Jesus. Jesus promises to be with us but asks us to be disciples and make disciples. What is a disciple? Father John Hardon defines it as, "One who is learning or has learned. In the New Testament the word describes any follower of Jesus' teaching."[107] We, as autistic disciples, are called to learn from Jesus and follow him.

As we go into the world, we need to share the love of Jesus as we can. Sure, it won't always be perfectly understood by others. I know most of us have had experiences where we tried to show love to another, but it was misunderstood, or where another was trying to love us, but we only realized it weeks later. Jesus wants us to be faithful in sharing his love: he is responsible for making it fruitful.

As autistic disciples, we will obviously learn in an autistic manner. Jesus didn't say, "Make yourself neurotypical then come to me," but, "Come to me as you are." As we are autistic, this is how we come to Jesus. Jesus doesn't transform us into being neurotypical but transforms us into autistic apostles.

---

107 Cf. Disciple at www.catholicculture.org/culture/library/dictionary.

Prayer

Lord, help me come to you. Help me to be your autistic disciple.

52. Missionaries to the Autistic World

Story

Often since I've been public about my diagnosis, I get messages or emails from parents trying to help their autistic children live the faith more fully. Often something seems obvious to me as an autistic Catholic priest that the parents never thought about as neurotypicals. Being autistic, I have a perspective from which, without even much effort, I can think of things that elude neurotypicals due to their different cognitive structures.

A few examples might include emphasizing logic over emotion when explaining the faith, or giving them a clear plan of what will happen in an upcoming prayer event so they can be prepared and not overload executive function. I might also explain that there is no sin in stepping out of Mass for two minutes if a sensory break is needed, and that stim toys or weighted blankets are perfectly fine to use in prayer or even Mass. These seem so obvious to me, yet parents trying to help their autistic children for years never thought of them. This shows a certain role we autistics have in evangelizing our fellow autistics.

Passage

As many of you as were baptized into Christ have put on Christ. There is neither Jew nor Greek, there is neither slave nor free, there is neither male nor female; for you are all one in Christ Jesus (Gal 3:27–28).

Reflection

We can easily add to Saint Paul: There is neither autistic nor neurotypical, but we are one in Christ Jesus. We are all called; however, the Gospel needs to be inculturated. As autism is a different brain structure, it is always going to be a different culture, and in many ways the difference is deeper and more dramatic than most cultural differences.

This book started by noting how much less likely autistics were to be regular church-attendees or even believers in God. Now, we come to the end and we see a call to go and change that. The evangelization of any culture starts from outside, but to be full and effective, it must involve the full understanding of those inside the culture.

In the first part, I noted how Dr. Ed Peters talked about Deaf Catholics being the best evangelizers in the Deaf community. In the autistic community, we autistics are the ones who can do the most to change how this community views God and participates in religion. We are the ones who speak autistic English, which, while it has the same basic meanings for English words, has a very different system of intonation, connotative meanings, and non-verbal communication.

If we each take our mission seriously, we will help change the narrative of the stereotypical autistic being an atheist. Autistics tend to be either atheists or serious about a religion. We don't get the social pressure to be semi-religious that happens to those who go to church a few times a year and kind of believe. We either believe or we don't. Those finishing this book can hopefully help some autistics move from non-belief to belief.

Prayer

Jesus, you want to speak to me and my fellow autistics in a way proper for us to understand. Help me share with my fellow autistics this joy of knowing you.

Appendix A

What Is Autism?

I THINK THAT most of my readers picking up this book already have a decent understanding of autism, but I figured a brief overview might be needed for some readers. If you live with this condition or have a family member who does, you probably already understand the basics. However, I can see religious professionals reading this book as their first book on autism.

Many conditions are characterized by a single trait. For example, someone who is Deaf can't hear or someone who is a paraplegic can't move his or her legs. Autism, however, is a combination of traits rather than just one. As a person needs some traits, but not all traits for a diagnosis, almost every trait that is observable externally is missing in some autistics. I think it is important to describe it both from outside using the standard diagnostic manual and from inside as people on the spectrum experience it.

According to the DSM-5, an autistic person should have some traits in at least three areas. The first area is: "Persistent deficits in social communication and social interaction across multiple

contexts."[108] This means, for example, not reading social cues, difficulties in eye contact, awkwardness in reciprocal communication,
difficulty maintaining relationships, or difficulty in speaking. This
last can be anything from the stereotypical flat affect to being non-
verbal. The second area is: "Restricted, repetitive patterns of
behavior, interests, or activities."[109] This criterion includes repetitive motor movements (stimming or flapping), insistence on
sameness, very obsessive or limited interests, hypersensitivity or
hyposensitivity, and fascination with certain light and movement.
This criterion indicates that an autistic person must have some of
these traits, and many of us don't manifest every aspect. The final
criterion makes sure that the prior two are properly attributed to
autism: they must be present from an early age (although they can
become more evident due to later situations), they must cause
impairment in ordinary life, and they must not be better explain-
able by intellectual disability.

The Autistic Self-Advocacy Network has a good summary of
autism from the perspective of autistic individuals rather than cli-
nicians. It begins, "Autism is a developmental disability that affects
how we experience the world around us. Autistic people are an
important part of the world. Autism is a normal part of life and
makes us who we are."[110] They note that we all experience autism

---

108 American Psychiatric Association and DSM-5 Task Force, *Diagnostic
and Statistical Manual of Mental Disorders: DSM-5* (Arlington, VA: American
Psychiatric Association, 2013), 50.

109 Ibid., 50.

110 Autistic Self Advocacy Network, "About Autism," Autistic Self Advocacy
Network, accessed May 22, 2020, https://autisticadvocacy.org/about-asan/
about-autism/.

differently, but have a few similarities. I summarize their list, adding in how I personally experience it.

— Autistics have different sensory processing. This might be that bright lights are painful or that we love it super bright. I think this is often a smaller range as I tend to like the brightest office but also am generally the first to put on sunglasses when outside. This can also be in how we like certain sensations like a weighted blanket, moving back and forth on a rocking chair, or repeated hand movements. Repeated actions are often called fidgeting by others, but we prefer stimming, as it is behavior done for the sensory stimulation provided—not due to nervousness as fidgeting often is. An autistic person who is over-stimulated will have a strong reaction such as a shutdown or meltdown. A meltdown may seem like a tantrum to some outside, but it is a non-voluntary response to being overwhelmed, while a tantrum is a voluntary act of trying to get one's way.

— Autistics think differently. This may include intense interests, oddities in focus, or executive functioning difficulties. Executive functioning involves decision-making, scheduling, planning activities, starting and finishing tasks, and organization. Executive functioning issues explain why we prefer routines. I personally don't need a precise routine, but I need a schedule in advance. Any change with a notice of less than forty-eight hours would create a significant challenge for me.

— Autistics move differently. Often, we have challenges with coordination or things like controlling voice volume. As noted above, had the DSM-5 existed in the 1980s, this issue would have led to a childhood diagnosis for me.

— Autistics communicate differently. This varies a lot, as some like me generally sound neurotypical at first, but then you might notice my intonation is just off "normal." Others have trouble speaking at all, so they use Augmentative and Alternative Communication (AAC), which takes various forms such as a picture board on their iPad.

— Autistics socialize differently. Most people get social rules subconsciously and they assume others do—so much so, that most neurotypicals can't even explain half the social rules but follow them without thinking. I can follow a lot of social rules, but in so doing, I'm making a conscious effort in things others do subconsciously. Other autistics have trouble even following social rules at all. In socializing, most people rely subconsciously on what is called theory of mind to intuit what the other person is feeling/thinking. We often have issues with intuiting what neurotypicals are feeling or thinking. Many of us can attest to being better able to "get" non-verbal cues when with fellow autistics than in the wider society.[111]

I think that both perspectives help us view autism from inside and outside. If we know what it is from outside, we can better recognize it. If we know what it is from inside, we can better sympathize with or help an autistic person. You will notice a fair amount of overlap in the definitions, but the external definition tends to focus more on relations with others while the internal definition focuses more on thinking and sensory differences. As the psychological definition is for diagnosing autism as a disorder,

---

111 Cf. Autistic Self Advocacy Network, "About Autism."

it focuses more on the negative aspects. On the other hand, the internal definition includes things that are neutral or positive as well. We might have a unique and unusual focus, but if we can parlay that into an academic or research career, that focus becomes a strength. Or for example, I think having to do theory of mind consciously helps me in posting online, as it is easier to bring something we consciously do in face-to-face conversation over to a social media post, than what is sub-conscious in face-to-face interaction.

Appendix B

Basic Catholic Prayers

The Sign of the Cross

In the name of the Father, and of the Son, and of the Holy Spirit. Amen.

Our Father

Our Father, who art in heaven, hallowed be thy name. Thy kingdom come, thy will be done, on earth as it is in heaven. Give us this day our daily bread, and forgive us our trespasses, as we forgive those who trespass against us, and lead us not into temptation, but deliver us from evil. Amen.

Hail Mary

Hail Mary, full of grace, the Lord is with thee. Blessed art thou among women, and blessed is the fruit of thy womb, Jesus. Holy Mary, Mother of God, pray for us sinners, now and at the hour of our death. Amen.

Glory Be

Glory be to the Father, and to the Son, and to the Holy Spirit, as it was in the beginning, is now, and ever shall be, world without end. Amen.

Jesus Prayer

Lord Jesus Christ, Son of the living God, have mercy on me, a sinner.

Apostles' Creed

I believe in God,
the Father almighty,
Creator of heaven and earth,
and in Jesus Christ, his only Son, our Lord,
who was conceived by the Holy Spirit,
born of the Virgin Mary,
suffered under Pontius Pilate,
was crucified, died, and was buried;
he descended into hell;
on the third day he rose again from the dead;
he ascended into heaven,
and is seated at the right hand of God the Father almighty;
from there he will come to judge the living and the dead.
I believe in the Holy Spirit,
the holy catholic Church,
the communion of saints,
the forgiveness of sins,

the resurrection of the body,
and life everlasting. Amen.

Prayer to the Holy Spirit

Come Holy Spirit, fill the hearts of your faithful and kindle in them the fire of your love.

Send forth your Spirit and they shall be created. And You shall renew the face of the earth.

O, God, who by the light of the Holy Spirit, did instruct the hearts of the faithful, grant that by the same Holy Spirit we may be truly wise and ever enjoy His consolations, Through Christ Our Lord, Amen.

Act of Contrition

O my God, I am heartily sorry for having offended you, and I detest all my sins, because of your just punishments, but most of all because they offend you, my God, who are all-good and deserving of all my love. I firmly resolve, with the help of your grace, to sin no more and to avoid the near occasions of sin.

Contrition can also be expressed in your own words, such as:

Jesus, I ask your forgiveness for my sins. I am sorry for offending you. Please help me to avoid all sin in the future.

Prayer to Saint Michael

Saint Michael, the Archangel, defend us in battle. Be our protection against the wickedness and snares of the devil. May God rebuke him, we humbly pray, and do thou, O Prince of the heavenly hosts, by the power of God, thrust into hell Satan and all the evil spirits who prowl about the world seeking the ruin of souls. Amen.

Angel of God

Angel of God, my Guardian dear, to whom God's love entrusts me here, ever this day be at my side, to light and guard, to rule and guide. Amen.

Hail, Holy Queen

Hail, holy Queen, Mother of mercy, our life, our sweetness, and our hope! To you do we cry, poor banished children of Eve. To you do we send up our sighs, mourning and weeping in this valley of tears. Turn then, most gracious advocate, your eyes of mercy toward us; and after this our exile, show unto us the blessed fruit of your womb, Jesus. O clement, O loving, O sweet Virgin Mary.

How to Pray the Rosary

Begin the Rosary by making the Sign of the Cross (p. 197); then, while holding the crucifix, pray the Apostles' Creed (p. 198). On the beads of the small chain pray one Our Father (p. 197), three Hail Marys (p. 197), and one Glory Be (p. 198). Next, announce the mystery and pray one Our Father, ten Hail Marys, and a Glory Be. This completes one decade. All the other decades are prayed in the same manner, while pondering the mystery for each decade. Pray the Hail, Holy Queen (p. 200) at the end.

1. Make the **Sign of the Cross** and pray the **Apostles' Creed.**
2. Pray the **Our Father.**
3. Pray 3 **Hail Marys.**
4. Pray the **Glory,** name the first Mystery, and pray the **Our Father.**
5. Pray 10 **Hail Marys.**
6. Pray the **Glory,** name the second Mystery, and pray the **Our Father.**
7. Repeat steps 5 and 6 with each Mystery until you reach the end.
8. Pray the **Glory** and the **Hail, Holy Queen.**

Joyful Mysteries

(Usually prayed on Mondays and Saturdays)

1. The Annunciation of the Angel to Mary
2. Mary Visits Her Cousin Elizabeth
3. The Birth of Jesus at Bethlehem
4. The Presentation of Jesus in the Temple
5. The Finding of Jesus in the Temple

Luminous Mysteries

(Usually prayed on Thursdays)

1. The Baptism of our Lord Jesus Christ
2. Jesus Reveals His Glory at the Wedding at Cana
3. Jesus Proclaims the Kingdom of God and Calls Us to Conversion
4. The Transfiguration of Jesus
5. The Institution of the Eucharist

Sorrowful Mysteries

(Usually prayed on Tuesdays and Fridays)

1. Jesus Prays in the Garden of Gethsemane
2. Jesus Is Scourged
3. Jesus Is Crowned with Thorns
4. Jesus Carries the Cross to Calvary
5. Jesus Is Crucified

GLORIOUS MYSTERIES

(Usually prayed on Wednesdays and Sundays)

1. Jesus Rises from the Dead
2. Jesus Ascends into Heaven
3. The Holy Spirit Descends on the Apostles
4. Mary Is Assumed into Heaven
5. Mary Is Crowned Queen of Heaven and Earth

Appendix C

Method of Mental Prayer

(For a fuller treatment of this method, see pages 26–30.)

1. Concentrate: I enter God's presence by setting aside other activities and concerns and calling to mind that I am going to converse with God. If I like, I can pray a particular vocal prayer that can begin this time of prayer.

2. Capture: In this stage, I grasp the material which I will be praying about during the meditation. I pick up the Bible or a spiritual book and read a section, and then go back over it slowly.

3. Consider: Now I move from simply reading a text to entering into it. For example, by using my senses to imagine the scene (from Scripture or the life of a saint), or by reflecting on a truth of the faith described in the passage.

4. Converse: Start a dialogue with Jesus to connect my meditation to my life. I might ask him questions, or consider whether he is asking something of me, or thank him for being close to me.

5. Commit: Now I make some small resolution from what I prayed about and offer it to Jesus.

6. Contemplate: I spend a good amount of time just being in God's presence, not thinking about a particular passage or asking God for anything, but just being there with him.

Appendix D

Advice for Autistic Penitents and Those Who Hear Their Confessions [112]

Autistics make up 1.5 to 2 percent of the population. I'm one of that group.

As awareness of autism grows, more pastoral sensitivity to our particular needs is also developing . . . even if slowly.

It is rare that we see information on how we autistics can best go about preparing and making our Confession, or how priests should hear our Confessions. We are not too radically different, but a few accommodations or adaptations can help us immensely in this sacrament.

---

112 This piece first appeared as: Fr. Matthew Schneider, LC, "An Autistic Priest with Advice for Autistic Penitents and Those Who Hear Their Confessions," Aleteia, October 23, 2019, https://aleteia.org/2019/10/23/an-autistic-priest -with-advice-for-autistic-penitents-and-those-who-hear-their-confessions/.

Since I've gone public about being autistic, I've gotten a number of questions from both autistics and priests about dealing with certain autism-specific situations in the confessional. I hope to provide a few quick pointers below for both sides of the screen.

Preliminary observations

The basic issue with autism is that our brains are wired differently from 98 percent of the population. In some things, this is advantageous: we often are great at long-term memory, detail-oriented work, or logic. However, it creates some difficulties. Much of the wiring issue is a lack of certain connections. For example, in the instant between you seeing someone and your conscious awareness of seeing them, your brain filters the images for facial expressions and social cues. That filter is lacking or weak for us autistics. Some of us have learned to compensate, consciously or semi-consciously, but the conscious filter takes a lot more work and usually is not as precise as the subconscious filter.

Many stereotypical autistic behaviors such as stimming (fidgeting, rocking, hand-flapping, etc.) are attempts to regulate our bodies due to how we receive emotional or sensory brain signals. When we have a meltdown or shutdown, this is not a willful action, but rather our brains simply shutting down due to overload, much like a car "overheating."

By adulthood, many of us have realized when this "overheating" is coming on, and what causes it, so with effort we can avoid the shutdown, or generally keep it less disruptive for others, with mechanisms such as hiding in our rooms. When I feel a shutdown coming on, for example, I go to my room and rock on my rocking chair with deep pressure for an hour, as I'm incapable of doing much else.

Realizing what is sinful

As sin requires a willed choice, we autistics need to become aware of the limitations due to our condition and not accuse ourselves of sin when our actions have been involuntary, or voluntary, but motivated by the recognition that a certain action might be needed in order to avoid something worse, even if it annoys those around us.

Misreading someone's emotions is not sinful unless we intentionally do it. Not looking someone in the eyes is not a sin, especially if this is necessary for self-regulation. Stimming is not a sin. Having a meltdown or shutdown is not a sin. Many times we don't even realize we are being rude, unless we are told so by others.

Nonetheless, we should attempt to cope with our condition in the most charitable way. For example, I used to stim by clicking a pen repeatedly, but several people told me that the sound annoyed them. Thus, I switched to a more silent stim that accomplishes the same goal.

Autistics often tend toward scruples, but as a fellow autistic who is also a moral theologian, let me give you a rule of thumb: If you're not sure if one of your autistic traits is willed, it probably isn't.

Unless we are intentionally rude, we are probably not at fault, so no need to confess it. Likewise, for priests hearing an autistic person's confession: you may have to explain to them that certain things—like unintentional rudeness—are not sins.

In the Confessional

As a fellow autistic, I'd generally recommend you start off by mentioning to the priest that you are autistic. Then, if he hears you confessing "lack of charity," such as "avoiding eye contact" or "annoying others with my actions," he can help you evaluate if in your case there is any lack of charity here. (Even for non-autistics, behaviors related to what is socially acceptable may not have any moral bearing, i.e., they are simply not sinful, even if they are not "socially acceptable.")

And by the way, fellow autistics, if you struggle with eye contact, I'd really recommend confession with a screen—so long as you don't need augmentative and alternative communication or something similar. Priests, please realize that autistics often find eye contact difficult or painful, so please don't insist on it. We tend to be honest to a fault, so we aren't looking away to deceive you.

Almost everyone gets nervous in confession. This includes autistics, but added to the regular nervousness is our extra sensory or social difficulties. This often leads us to stim more during the sacrament, to regulate these emotions and sensory issues. If you are autistic, have no fear about stimming in the confessional. Priests, please just realize that stimming is a natural part of being autistic and don't worry.

Some will have challenges speaking. The Church teaches that the penitent must communicate—not specifically speak—their sins to the priest, so using a written note or other non-verbal communication works. Some will have a laptop equipped with pictures for AAC (augmentative and alternative communication). If you are autistic, don't feel bad handing the priest a note or typing on AAC if you can't talk, even if you are verbal at other times. Some autistics also know sign language. (However, most priests don't know sign, so you may need an interpreter who is bound to the seal as strictly as the priest. I've started to learn sign to help people who need it for confession, but I am far from being able to understand a confession in sign.)

Some who have low functional IQ or extreme communication issues will need to use a visual list of sins where the priest can ask, "Did you X?" while pointing to a picture of X, to which the autistic penitent can nod or shake his or her head.

Priests: If anything comes up where you need to question an autistic penitent, please be concrete and/or illustrate what you mean with an example. "Did you want what someone else had so badly that you wished it was taken from them?" is far clearer to us than "Were you jealous?"

While this limited space doesn't allow me to go into more, I hope this initial advice can help both autistics and those who hear their Confessions. I am not omniscient, but being one of the few who is both a priest and autistic, I think I have something unique to offer on this question!

One final recommendation: As autistics tend to be anxious—they have an anxiety diagnosis at a much higher rate than the general population—advice on how to deal with anxiety is usually also helpful.

Pauline
BOOKS & MEDIA

A mission of the Daughters of St. Paul

As apostles of Jesus Christ,
evangelizing today's world:

We are CALLED to holiness
by God's living Word and Eucharist.

We COMMUNICATE the Gospel message
through our lives and through all
available forms of media.

We SERVE the Church
by responding to the hopes and needs
of all people with the Word of God,
in the spirit of St. Paul.

For more information visit our Web site:
www.pauline.org

BOOKS & MEDIA

The Daughters of St. Paul operate book and media centers at the following addresses. Visit, call, or write the one nearest you today, or find us at www.paulinestore.org.

¡También somos su fuente para libros,
videos y música en español!